W9-BFC-076

THE HEALTHY *Fiesta*

Jacqueline Higuera McMahan

THE OLIVE PRESS

COPYRIGHT 1990 BY
JACQUELINE HIGUERA MCMAHAN
All rights reserved
No part of this publication may be reproduced
or transmitted in any form or by any means, electronic or
mechanical, including photocopy recording, or any infor-
mation storage and retrieval system without permission in
writing from the publisher.

Requests for permission to make copies of any part
of this work should be mailed to:
THE OLIVE PRESS, P.O. BOX 194, LAKE HUGHES, CA
93532

Book Design: Robert McMahan
Cynthia Kincaid
Cover photography: Joe Lingrey
Robert McMahan

LIBRARY OF CONGRESS CATALOG CARD NUMBER

ISBN: 0-9612150-9-7

FIRST PRINTING, APRIL, 1990
SECOND PRINTING, APRIL, 1991

Printed in the United States of America

To Dad

**who ate all my early failures without complaint
and taught me never to give up.**

Previous books by Jacqueline Higuera McMahan

California Rancho Cooking, 1983
The Salsa Book, 1986
The Red and Green Chile Book, 1987
The Salsa Book (Revised Edition) 1989

The recipes in this book have been nutritionally analyzed by Hill Nutrition Associates, Inc. My thanks go to Lynne and Bill Hill for excellent work, patience, and humor.

The analysis given at the end of each recipe is per serving. If for reasons of health you are concerned about any sodium listed in a recipe, please delete. To compute calories derived from the grams of fat given per serving, multiply 9 x amount of fat grams.

For instance, 5 grams of fat would equal 45 calories.

CONTENTS

INTRODUCTION

come from a family where food is more than sustenance and holds greater meaning beyond the counting of calories. When a Spanish-Californian, particularly one of my uncles, described a meal his words were not only poetical but commentative. The sweet basil was a fragrant touch but the dish had too much pepper. The cooking of the food had to be done in a particular way. Even if just beans and tortillas were being served it was done with ceremony. And then the discussion was relished. This was all part of the romance we had with food and the romance that I still have. After a great dinner when all the guests have left, there is that moment I enjoy with my husband amidst the empty wine glasses and crumbs. We sit at the table with a last cup of expresso. He tells me what he loved and I tell him that the vegetables needed more basil and the fish was cooked five minutes too long but I loved the sauce. This exchange is our private ritual of savoring the memory of food even after its gone.

1

This love affair with food and my occupation as a cookbook writer have both contributed considerable calories toward my survival. In fact, more than I needed. About three years ago, I realized I could not continue eating my way through life as I once did. My friends and many of the people I talked to were experiencing the same indignation. There is a lot of food out there— saucer-sized chocolate chip cookies, giant muffins and cinnamon rolls, Dove bars, and more. But if you eat it, it will get you. Eventually. But all of those temptations have nothing to do with savoring food. There's eating and there's savoring.

The satisfaction food is the stuff of this book. We will not discuss diets here because I am not qualified for that since I have only gone off diets. What counts is to eat food that is at once healthy but brings joy to your tastebuds. For me, that means spice. Garlic. Chiles. And more garlic and chiles. Since I grew up with the cooking of a Spanish-California mother, I have turned to Latin and Southwestern foods for answers. This style of food is particularly adaptable to healthy eating be- cause it emphasizes an abundance of carbohydrates, vegetables, and smaller amounts of meat. The spices trick your palate into a form of contentment.

At first I hesitated when faced with the task of turning Mexican recipes around, minus a lot of calories. I let a whole summer escape me while I did everything but work on the recipes. Finally when September came, I began with the soup chapter. I started with Hugo's Caldo de Tlalpeño mainly because I was mad at Hugo for not giving me the recipe. When I figured it out I was so ecstatic I went on to the next recipe and the next. Each soup had such an abundance of flavor with a minimum of the usual fats that it even amazed me. I had previously assumed that sauteeing had to be done with a couple of tablespoons of olive oil. When I used a teaspoon of oil, everything still worked and tasted just as good. Momentum started to build.

The further I worked on extracting extraneous fats from traditional Latin recipes, the more I became a believer in the cause I had adopted. I cursed the cause before I loved it. I had to part with my bad habits, which I had become attached to, before I could see that good habits taste just as good.

Besides, there are days when you can still have your cake. Just think about it carefully. And savor it.

SALADS

CHAPTER I

SALADS INSPIRED IN CALIFORNIA AND MEXICO

side from being health conscious or calorie conscious, most of us love a beautiful salad. It can be appealing to the eye and satisfy our primitive need for something to chew on. But at home, making salad is regretfully a neglected art form. Many cooks expend their energy on the main dish or company dessert, leaving the salad to be thrown together at the last minute (with bottled dressing). A salad can serve as an entire lunch or dinner if it contains bits of protein, vegetables, pasta, beans, homemade croutons or tortilla chips. Many of the young chefs, out to be inventive, are defying tradition. A salad has to start out with greens but from there anything goes: grilled meats or seafood are added, maybe warm dressing instead of cold, combinations of raw and cooked vegetables, barely cooked beans, fresh herbs and edible flowers. Dressings are the culprits. They carry the fat calories and you need to use as little dressing as possible.

THE TRICKS FOR MAKING GREAT SALADS

Use flavorful, dark green lettuces such as romaine, red leaf, or some of the unusual field lettuces cultivated in temperate regions of the country. If you like iceberg lettuce, use it for its crunchiness rather than for the entire salad. Lettuce is mostly water so the tendency is to add flavor by pouring on the dressing.

A great salad deserves a great dressing. Buy the best, most flavorful oils and vinegars that you can find. I buy red wine vinegar, from a small winery in the Santa Cruz Mountains (see Resources), which pairs wonderfully with good olive oil. Just because an olive oil is marked virgin does not mean that it is exceptional in taste. A good test for an olive oil: does it have a delicate flavor of olives? I use the Italian Olio Sasso and the Spanish Ibarra because they are light but flavorful and theprice does not require a second mortgage. A more intense oil, such as Badia a Coltibuono can be added in droplets to the Ibarra or Olio Sasso when doing a Caesar Salad. When making a vinaigrette for a tostada salad, the lighter olive oils are best If your dressing is made with great tasting ingredients, you will need less to coat your salad greens. Using a trick learned from a health spa, I stick my dinner fork into a little bowl of homemade vinai-grette and use what's clinging to the fork to toss the salad on my plate. You can allow yourself a couple of stabs of dressing. If there are pools of dressing at the bottom of your plate or salad bowl, you have added too much but you will learn with practice.

The next suggestion is something so simple you may not become a believer until you try it. **Dry your lettuce completely.** After you wash your lettuce and spin it in a lettuce-drier or pat it with a tea towel, lay it out on sturdy paper towels and pat it dry. Since dressing slides off wet leaves, you will tend to add more to a bowl of slippery greens. My friend Michael, a consummate lettuce drier and jazz tuba player (perhaps the two crafts are interrelated) approaches lettuce drying like an art. His salads are like bouquets of greenery floating in the salad bowl. Michael's drying ritual usually provides a lot of in-house joking among dinner guests but after one bite of salad, seasoned gently with droplets of Dijon dressing, they are converts. I often wash and dry my lettuce, wrap in paper towels and store in a zip-loc bag in the refrigerator for up to 3 days.

To eliminate the need for too much dressing, **add flavor and crunch to your salad greens with varying textures.** Keep on hand ingredients like Jalapeño Carrots (see page 19), crisp red bell peppers, homemade croutons from interesting breads and good cheeses like Asiago which can add flavor even when used in small amounts. Cooked beans like garbanzos, kidney beans, and black beans add a nice bite along with nourishment so I always try to keep some canned beans in my pantry to use for spur of the moment inspirations. Sometimes I cook up some green beans, asparagus, or spinach macaroni (tossed with a little olive oil and vinegar so it does not become sticky) to chill and add later to salads. Since you eat with your eyes besides your taste buds, a plate of greens with colorful tidbits will keep you away from overdoing the dressing.

TURKEY CHIPOTLE TOSTADA

This is a good recipe to make with leftover turkey or you can use turkey tenderloins. Marinate in a little olive oil, lemon juice, garlic, and cilantro and grill or broil them. I often do this if I anticipate the having to prepare many salads, tostadas, or sandwiches for weekend guests or my own ravenous teenage sons.

2 turkey tenderloins, about 12 ounces each
1 tablespoon olive oil, 3 tablespoons lemon juice, 2
*   cloves minced garlic, and 1 tablespoon snipped*
*   cilantro= 1/4 cup marinade*

1/2 head of romaine, washed, dried, and torn
Pickled red onion rings, see recipe below or regular red
  onion, sliced
8 cherry tomatoes, washed and halved
A heaping 1/2 cup shredded mozzarella cheese
1/4 cup cilantro, snipped with scissors
6 flour tortillas (7")

Chipotle dressing: Makes 3/4 cup
1/4 cup mayonnaise
1/2 cup nonfat yogurt
Juice from 1 lime
1 clove garlic, minced through press
1 canned chipotle chile
1 teaspoon adobo sauce from can

1. Place all ingredients for dressing in food processor and blend. This is also a good spread for sandwiches and inside pita bread with chicken and turkey. The dressing is spicy hot so just add 1 chile and no more until you taste for heat level.

2. If you are using the turkey tenderloins marinate them for at least 1 hour and then grill or broil for about 9 minutes on each side. Slice the filets into strips or shred leftover turkey if that is what you are using.

3. Toast 6 flour tortillas in a preheated 375 degree oven for about 8 minutes or until they are crisp around the edges. Watch carefully.

4. Spread 1 tablespoon of chipotle dressing on each

tortilla. Lay on a few pieces of turkey (2 ounces). Sprinkle with the torn lettuce. Arrange the pickled onion slices and cherry tomatoes over the top. Drizzle each tostada with a couple of teaspoons more of chipotle dressing and sprinkle each with 1 tablespoon of mozzarella cheese and a bit of cilantro.

Note: you can lower the calories even more by using reduced fat mozzarella cheese.
Serves 6.

Calories	381	Protein	34 gm
Fat	13 gm	Carbohydrate	29 gm
Sodium	478 gm	Cholesterol	85 mg

PICKLED PINK ONIONS
FOR TOSTADAS, TACOS, AND ENCHILADAS

Often in Mexico, when you are served enchiladas or tacos, they are topped with pickled vegetables-pink onions or maybe a mixture of diced carrots and new potatoes, giving a flavor boost to even the simplest offering.

2 medium red onions, sliced
1 cup vinegar
1/2 cup water
1 tablespoon olive oil
2 teaspoons oregano
1 bay leaf
5 crushed peppercorns

Simmer all the ingredients except the sliced onions in a saucepan until brought to a boil. Immediately pour over the red onions in a heatproof bowl and allow them to steep for a least 1 hour. They will turn a pretty pink color which is the main reason for using the red onions. Stored in a jar in the refrigerator they will keep well for a month. Makes 1 pint.

Calories	34 gm	Protein	.51 gm
Fat	2 gm	Carbohydrate	5 gm
Sodium	1 mg	Cholesterol	0

CHICKEN TOSTADA WITH GRAPE SALSA

I could not resist making grape salsa for this particular tostada because it uses a combination of ingredients often found in chicken salads.

Grape Salsa:

2 cups seedless flame, purple, or Thompson grapes, sliced in half
1 tablespoon lemon juice
1 tablespoon rice vinegar
1 teaspoon olive oil
1 clove garlic, minced through press
1 fresh jalapeño chile, seeded, finely minced
2 tablespoon chives, snipped
2 tablespoons cilantro, snipped with scissors
4 tablespoons toasted almond slivers, crushed
1/8 teaspoon salt

1/8 teaspoon cayenne pepper
1/4 teaspoon freshly ground pepper

1. Stir all the ingredients together and allow to season for at least 1 hour before serving. It's also fun to use different colors of grapes for this salsa.

Serves 6

Calories	71	Protein	1 gm
Fat	4 gm	Carbohydrate	9 gm
Sodium	25 mg	Cholesterol	0

Perfect Poached Chicken Breasts:

1 and 1/2 skinned chicken breasts (about 24 ounces)
2 cans chicken broth (14 ounces each of reduced
  sodium broth)
Juice of 1 lemon

1. Bring chicken to a simmer in the liquid. Turn to low heat and cook gently for 15 minutes. Remove from heat and allow to cool in the broth until liquid is just tepid. Reserve broth for another use. When chicken is cool enough to handle, remove from the bones and cut into strips.

Tostadas:

Poached or grilled chicken, cut into strips
6 small flour tortillas
1 tablespoon oil
3 cups washed and dried romaine lettuce, chopped

1/2 cup light sour cream (40% less fat)
1 tablespoon frozen apple juice concentrate

1.   Brush the tortillas lightly with oil and bake in a preheated 375 degree oven until they are crisp, about 8 minutes. Watch carefully.

2. Stir together the sour cream and frozen apple juice for dressing.

3.   Place the crisp tortillas on 6 plates and cover with shredded lettuce, about 1/4 cup chicken, and a couple of tablespoons of grape salsa. Drizzle a tablespoon of the light sour cream dressing over the top.

Serves 6 as a light lunch.

Calories	260	Protein	30 gm
Fat	8 gm	Carbohydrate	15 gm
Sodium	276 mg	Cholesterol	72 mg

PASADENA CHICKEN TOSTADA SALAD

 Frequently, I will eat something in a restaurant and want to recreate it at at home. Many times over, I have ordered the Chicken Tostada Salad at the Parkway Grill in Pasadena and I think this salad comes very close to the restaurant's although they use their own smoked chicken and the chef's dressing contains more virgin olive oil. Consider this an entire meal!

18 ounces of boned, skinned chicken breast

Marinade of 1/4 cup lime juice, 1 tablespoon olive oil, 1 tablespoon reduced sodium soy sauce, 1 teaspoon ground chile, 1 tablespoon brown sugar

1 and 1/2 cups cooked black beans (see recipe below)

1 and 1/2 cups corn kernels from fresh corn

1/2 head of romaine lettuce, washed and dried

1/2 head of red leaf lettuce, washed and dried

1 and 1/2 cups shredded reduced-fat Monterey Jack cheese or part-skim Mozzarella

4 corn tortillas, cut into triangles

2 avocados mashed with the juice of 1/2 lemon, 1 canned jalapeño chile, and some juice from the can, 1 minced clove of garlic, and a pinch of salt.

8 cherry tomatoes, washed and halved

Herb Dressing

1 tablespoon balsamic vinegar

2 tablespoons white wine vinegar

2 teaspoons Dijon mustard

1 clove garlic

3/4 cup sliced celery (about 1 and 1/2 stalks)

1/4 cup water

1/4 cup olive oil

1 teaspoon each dried oregano and basil

1 tablespoon fresh chives, snipped

1. Pound the boned chicken between waxed paper until flattened. This will help the chicken cook evenly.

Marinate for at least 1 hour. Grill or broil the chicken for about 3 minutes per side or until done. Set aside.

2. Puree dressing in food processor. Wash lettuce. Wrap in paper towels and chill in tightly closed plastic bags. Shred the cheese.

3. Brush the triangles of tortilla with oil and toast on a cookie sheet in a preheated 375 degree oven for about 10 minutes or until crisp.

4. Steam the corn kernels over simmering water for 3 minutes. Set aside.
Drain the cooked black beans. If they are cold from the refrigerator, warm them.

5. Make the guacamole at the last minute and get ready to assemble the tostada salads. Tear the salad greens, cut the grilled chicken into strips, and arrange the rest of the ingredients in front of you. You can let your guests make their own salads. Present all the ingredients in pretty bowls for them to choose their preferences. You can show the way by making the first salad.

The Presentation Cover each plate with a couple of cups of torn greens. Sprinkle each salad with about 1/4 cup corn, 1/4 cup black beans, 2 tablespoons of herb dressing, and 1/4 cup cheese. Lay a pinwheel design of grilled chicken around the top of everything. Add a dollop of guacamole to the center and decorate with cherry tomato halves. Poke the crisp tortillas around the guacamole. They're ready to eat. Pass the herb dressing for anyone that needs more.

This salad serves 8

```
Calories 409          Protein       27 gm
Fat       21 gm       Carbohydrate 31 gm
Sodium   417 mg       Cholesterol  49 mg
```

BLACK BEANS FOR SALADS AND TOSTADAS

For a salad you want the beans to be firmer and appetizingly black so they do not require a presoaking or long cooking time. If you need beans in large amounts, just double the recipe. Black beans can also be pressure-cooked in 30 minutes. The beans freeze quite well.

1 cup or 1/2 pound black beans
4 cups water
1/2 cup chopped onion
2 cloves garlic
1/2 teaspoon salt

1. Rinse beans off in cold, running water and search for stones. Place in a 2-quart pot and cover with 4 cups water and rest of ingredients except the salt. Adding the salt too early can cause the beans to remain hard. Simmer on low for about 1 and 1/2 hours. Add the salt during the last 15 minutes. Check on the beans and taste them as you want them to be cooked and yet firm.

6 servings

```
Calories 135          Protein        8 gm
Fat       .56 gm      Carbohydrate 25 gm
Sodium   185 mg       Cholesterol    0
```

ELEGANT TACO SALAD

Taco salads seem to be a California phenomenon reaching all levels from the bag of Fritos, chile beans, and chopped iceberg to haute taco salads with lobster. I love them all. This one is in between and is suggested for a simple backyard picnic along with a dessert of home-made cookies and iced tea.

Jalapeño Vinaigrette:

3 tablespoons red wine vinegar
3 tablespoons lemon juice
1/4 cup water
3 tablespoons olive oil
1 teaspoon Dijon mustard
1 clove garlic, minced through a press
1 tomato, juiced and seeded
1 pickled jalapeño chile
1/4 cup cilantro
Freshly ground black pepper
1/4 teaspoon salt

1. Using a food processor, blend vinegar, lemon juice, water, olive oil, mustard and garlic until thickened. Then add pieces of tomato, chile, and cilantro. Blend until just tiny bits of chile and cilantro show. I use this vinaigrette frequently with tossed salads and vegetables. Makes 1 and 1/4 cup dressing.
10 servings

Calories	41	Protein	.14 gm
Fat	4 gm	Carbohydrate	1 gm
Sodium	93mg	Cholesterol	0

Taco Salad:

2 teaspoons olive oil
1 pound ground sirloin
1 teaspoon each dried oregano and basil
2 teaspoons ground chile powder
1 teaspoon cumin seed, crushed
6 corn tortillas, cut into wedges
1 tablespoon olive oil
1 head of romaine lettuce, washed and dried
Several rings of pink, marinated onion
*1 and 1/2 cups grated reduced-fat Cheddar or
    mozzarella cheese*
*Garnish: cherry tomatoes, black olives, pickled
    jalapeño chile, or slices of Jalapeño Carrots*

1. Saute the meat in the olive oil, sprinkling with spices as it cooks. Drain the sauteed meat on paper towels. Pat to remove all fat.

2. Place tortilla wedges on a baking sheet and brush with olive oil. Bake in a preheated 375 degree oven 8-10 minutes or until golden and crisp.

3. Just before serving, tear up the romaine and toss with enough of the Jalapeño Vinaigrette to barely moisten it. Also toss in just 1/2 cup of the grated cheese.

4. Lastly add the cooked spiced meat, the tortilla wedges, and the pickled onion rings.

5. Place a serving on each plate. Sprinkle with more cheese and add any of the garnishes such as cherry tomatoes, olives, or Jalapeño Carrot slices.

6 servings

Calories	439	Protein	24 gm
Fat	30 gm	Carbohydrate	16 gm
Sodium	304 mg	Cholesterol	74 mg

JALAPEÑO CARROTS

I am mad about these carrots and put them in everything from tuna salad sandwiches to salads such as the taco salad above. In Mexico they eat them with cheese as an appetizer. This recipe is lower in calories than the original which called for quite a bit more olive oil.

2 bunches of carrots (about 2 pounds), peeled
1 and 1/2 cups apple cider vinegar
3/4 cup water
2 tablespoons olive oil
1 bay leaf
1 onion, sliced thinly
5-8 canned jalapeño chiles, some seeds removed

1. Cut carrots into 3-inch diagonal pieces.

2. Place in a vegetable steamer, bring to a simmer, and steam for exactly 6 minutes. The carrots must remain crisp or they lose their charm.

3. While the carrots are steaming, pour all the rest of the

ingredients into a bowl. Dump the hot carrots into the marinade. While the carrots are cooling, keep stirring them in the marinade. They need at least a couple of hours to for the flavors to penetrate. Store them in a glass jar. Serve them on a bed of parsley or cilantro accompanied by sticks of sharp cheese or use them in everything like I do.

10 servings for appetizers

Calories 69	Protein	1 gm
Fat 3 gm	Carbohydrate	11 gm
Sodium 171 mg	Cholesterol	0

DELICIOUS LOW-CLASS TACO SALAD

This is the kind of salad you can bring to a barbecue or a potluck and everyone will ask you for the recipe. Aside from gourmet dishes it always amazes me how people love fun food. It is leaner than most popular versions and I had to include it because of some kind of perverse loyalty.

Taco Salad:

1 head of iceberg lettuce, washed, dried, and chopped
1 pound lean hamburger (15 %)
l can kidney beans, 15 ounces, drained
2 cups corn chips (low-salt preferable)
2 medium tomatoes, quartered
1 red onion, sliced
1 cup pitted black olives
1 and 1/2 cups grated Cheddar cheese (reduced-fat if possible)

1. Wash and dry the lettuce and fry the hamburger. Drain well.

6 servings

Calories	417	Protein	25 gm
Fat	25 gm	Carbohydrate	22 gm
Sodium	582 mg	Cholesterol	66 mg

Guacamole Dressing:

1 ripe avocado

1 tablespoon lemon juice

1 teaspoon hot pepper sauce

1 clove garlic, minced in press

3 green onions, cut into pieces

1/2 cup plain nonfat yogurt or sour cream

2 tablespoons bottled Mexican green sauce

3 teaspoons dry Ranch dressing for flavoring

1. Place everything in a food processor and blend well. If you are being authentic you will have to use sour cream for the dressing but if calories are your concern, try using nonfat yogurt. Makes 1 and 1/2 cups or 6 servings.

2. Assembling the salad: toss the lettuce, hamburger, kidney beans, olives, cheese, corn chips, and onion together in a huge bowl. Drizzle the Guacamole Dressing over everything. Garnish with the tomato quarters and more black olives.

6 servings

Calories	36	Protein	1 gm
Fat	3 gm	Carbohydrate	2 gm
Sodium	119 mg	Cholesterol	.5 mg

THE CAPTAIN'S CAESAR SALAD

This salad enjoys a Mexican birthright, having been created by Caesar Cardini in Tijuana and is now recreated the world over.

One of the best unauthentic Caesar Salads I ever ate was on a 62 foot ketch anchored in a small cove off one of the British Virgin Islands. The captain was in a testy mood because the dinghy had a new leak and he informed us we would be spending the night before moving on. Molly, the cook poked her head out of the hatch to inform him she was not spending the night because it was much better to go on to Cooper's Island, a better anchorage. In between mouthfuls of Caesar Salad the captain told the cook that he knew where to go and when. The cook told the captain that she knew where he should go. She didn't mean Cooper's Island. We leaned back, sipping the icy margarita that Molly had handed us when we came dripping out of the salty water. The captain told Molly he would take away her passport and throw her off the boat for insubordination. We all protested. No one could make a Caesar Salad like Molly. We took the captain aside and asked him a question we all knew the answer to, "Can you cook?" He looked at the leaky dinghy, which was less than Captain Bly himself had. We went on to Cooper's Island where Molly served Lobster Curry for dinner and we all wore fresh T-shirts and toasted the captain for knowing a good cook never gives up the ship.

2 heads of romaine lettuce
2 cloves garlic, minced through press
2 teaspoons anchovy paste
2 teaspoons Dijon mustard
1 and 1/2 teaspoons Worcestershire sauce
1/4 teaspoon freshly ground black pepper
2 tablespoons lemon juice (1 lemon)
1/3 cup good flavorful olive oil
2 tablespoons + 1/4 cup Parmesan cheese
1 and 1/2 cups cubed French bread for croutons
1 clove garlic, minced with a press
1 tablespoon olive oil

1. Wash the lettuce, pulling off the outer leaves and reserving for another salad. Use the hearts of each romaine for this salad as it is most delicious if you eat with your fingers. You do not want huge leaves. Dry each leaf well with paper towels.

2. Blend the anchovy paste into the minced garlic. Then beat in the mustard, Worcestershire sauce, pepper, lemon juice, and olive oil. Blend in the tablespoon of Parmesan. This will help thicken the dressing so that it clings to the lettuce. Molly coddled an egg for 1 minute and then beat just the yolk into the dressing. Since we are concerned about cutting back on fats and cholesterol this step is eliminated.

3. To prepare homemade croutons, cut the bread in 1-inch slices and then dice. Place on a cookie sheet. Combine the minced clove of garlic and 1 tablespoon of

olive oil. Brush on croutons. Bake in a preheated 375 degree oven until golden, about 10 minutes. Watch carefully. Stir the croutons once so they bake evenly.

4. Drizzle part of dressing over the greens, placed in a large, wide salad bowl. Lift up the greens gently, adding more dressing and the croutons. Sprinkle liberally with the grated cheese and serve.
Serves 6.

Calories	219	Protein	7 gm
Fat	17 gm	Carbohydrate	11 gm
Sodium	407 mg	Cholesterol	6 mg

WARM SPAGHETTI SALAD WITH COLD SALSA

When I want something beautiful, easy and good, this is what I serve. The contrast of the warm pasta with the cold salsa is one of the best.   This spaghetti was frantically invented while we still lived in Queretaro, Mexico when I was spending one of those leisurely, lazy afternoons doing nothing. There was a loud knock on the door and my maid, Pueblito came to tell me that there were six elegantes (well-dressed people) standing out-side to see me. My husband, the director of a private school, had invited visiting student teachers from Pennsylvania to an early dinner and forgotten to tell me. They thanked me for the invitation as they had heard reports that I was a gourmet cook. I thought of various way to murder my husband. After tucking them into the sala, I sprinted for the kitchen and sent Pueblito running out the backdoor chanting Madre de Dios to see if the neighbors had any spaghetti. Pueblito, usually not known for speed, was back in minutes with two packages of spaghetti. I found 5 ripe tomatoes, garlic, chiles, a wedge of Parmesan cheese, and one can of smoked sturgeon. Hurriedly, we made a salsa fresca and starting boiling the spaghetti. My husband came in the door looking sheepish but having too many witnesses, I couldn't do anything to him YET. With great flourish, the spaghetti was tossed at the table with olive oil, salsa, grated Parmesan cheese and several grinds of fresh pepper. The guests thought it was an old Mexican recipe and my husband has never repeated his folly.

Salsa Fresca:

4 ripe tomatoes, diced with skins on
1 clove garlic, minced through press
1 jalapeño chile, seeded and minced
1/2 cup red onion, diced
1/2 cup red or green bell pepper
1 tablespoons red wine vinegar
1 teaspoon olive oil
Freshly ground pepper and salt to taste
2 tablespoons cilantro, snipped with scissors, optional

1. Dice up everything and stir together. Refrigerate the salsa, if possible for a least an hour before serving it with the spaghetti.

Calories	33	Protein	1 gm
Fat	1 gm	Carbohydrate	6gm
Sodium	7 mg	Cholesterol	0

The Spaghetti:

1 pound dried spaghetti
2 tablespoon olive oil
1 clove garlic, minced through a press
1 teaspoon Tabasco
1/2 cup grated Parmesan Reggiano cheese
Freshly ground black pepper to taste
Red pepper flakes to taste

1. Add the garlic and Tabasco to the olive oil and warm in a little pan or measuring cup. Set aside.

2. Bring a pot of water to a boil and add the spaghetti. Cook until it is al dente, about 8 to 10 minutes. Drain. Do not rinse.

3 To serve: immediately place the hot spaghetti on a platter and toss with the warm olive oil. Toss with the salsa fresca, the grated Parmesan, and some freshly grated black pepper. Pass more grated cheese and red pepper flakes at the table. Serves 4 to 6 people depending upon whether or not you are offering salad and bread (or a can of sturgeon).
6 servings

Calories	358	Protein	13 gm
Fat	8 gm	Carbohydrate	56 gm
Sodium	162 mg	Cholesterol	6 mg

JICAMA AND RED PEPPER SALAD

Originally I came up with this recipe for The *Salsa Book*. It is an example of how easily a chopped salsa can become a salad and I could not resist including it in this chapter. Its crunchiness is a perfect compliment to Southwestern foods and I would choose it any day over the more traditional Christmas salad of jicama, oranges, and beets. It's also a great diet salad if you cut the oil down to the barest minimum of a couple of teaspoons.

1 small jicama (1 pound), peeled
3 carrots, peeled
1 red bell pepper
1 small red onion, peeled
1 to 2 jalapeño chiles, seeded
2 cloves garlic, minced through a press
1/2 cup rice vinegar
2 tablespoons canola oil or olive oil
1/4 teaspoon freshly ground black pepper
1/2 teaspoon crushed red pepper flakes
2 teaspoons dried oregano
Pinch of salt
3 to 4 tablespoons cilantro, snipped with scissors

1. Dice the vegetables into equal sizes.

2. Whisk together the garlic, rice vinegar, oil, black and red pepper, oregano, salt, and cilantro. Pour the dressing over the vegetables and marinate for at least 2 hours

before serving. Use the minimum amount of oil if you are watching your intake of fats.

Serves 6 as an accompaniment or side dish.

Calories	97	Protein	2 gm
Fat	5 gm	Carbohydrate	13 gm
Sodium	43 mg	Cholesterol	0

BASQUE SALAD

In Arizona, Nevada, and, California there are small communities with Basque hotels serving families, sheepherders, and trenchermen who know about the good food. It is my style of food because they use a lot of garlic. This refreshing salad is similar to the Greek-style salad, the only difference being that the Basque cooks use goat cheese instead of feta. With a hunk of rough bread, I have often made a meal out of just this salad.

2 ripe tomatoes, diced (2 cups)
1 cucumber, peeled, diced (1 cup)
1 red onion, peeled and chopped (1 cup)
1 red or green bell pepper, diced (1 cup)
1 clove garlic, minced through a press
2 tablespoons red wine vinegar
2 teaspoons dried oregano
Pinch of salt
1/2 teaspoon black pepper
2 tablespoons flavorful olive oil
1/2 cup crumbled mild goat cheese or feta cheese
* (4 ounces)*

1. Combine all the diced vegetables with the dressing ingredients and the crumbled cheese. It is best if it marinates together for at least 1 hour.

6 servings

Calories	85	Protein	3 gm
Fat	6 gm	Carbohydrate	6 gm
Sodium	86 mg	Cholesterol	9 mg

PEAR SALAD

In wintertime when I want a refreshing change I often turn to this salad. Everyone seems to love the combination and I never make enough.

1 head of red leaf lettuce, washed
2 cups of washed spinach leaves
3 pears
1 cup roughly chopped walnuts, toasted
1/2 cup crumbled blue cheese or Roquefort cheese
1/3 cup raspberry vinegar
1/2 teaspoon dry mustard
1/2 teaspoon freshly ground pepper
1/2 teaspoon sugar
2 teaspoons walnut oil
2 tablespoons light oil

1. Dry the lettuce and spinach until completely dry and fluffy. Wrap in a tea towel and then in a plastic bag until needed.

2. Toast the walnuts for only 8 minutes in a 350 degree oven until they are only very lightly toasted. Set aside.

3. Mix up the raspberry vinegar, dry mustard, pepper, sugar, walnut oil, and light oil.

4. Just before serving time, tear up the lettuce and spinach and place in a bowl. Peel the pears, core, and cut into paper-thin slices. Crumble in the blue cheese and walnuts. Toss the salad with the dressing, adding the pear slices, Reserve a few slices for garnish. Serves 6.

Calories	286	Protein	7 gm
Fat	22 gm	Carbohydrate	20 gm
Sodium	177 mg	Cholesterol	8 mg

TEXAS POPPYSEED DRESSING
WITH GRAPEFRUIT, ORANGE, AND
AVOCADO SALAD

For many years, Helen Corbitt directed the restaurants for Neiman-Marcus in Dallas, Texas and The Greenhouse spa. She was amused that, with all of her accomplishments in the food business, she should be famous for a poppyseed dressing. Even those big Texas men loved the dressing but Helen was taken aback when she saw them putting it on their potatoes.

Below is an adaptation of Helen Corbitt's original recipe minus a hefty dose of sugar. This dressing is great over fruit salads such as this one. At times, I have even added slices of strawberries.

POPPYSEED DRESSING:

1/4 cup chopped onion (preferably red)
1 teaspoon dry mustard
1/4 teaspoon salt
1/2 teaspoon celery seeds
1 and 1/2 tablespoons poppy seeds
1/4 cup brown sugar
1/3 cup cider vinegar (do not use wine vinegar)
2 tablespoons lemon juice (1 lemon)
2/3 cup mild oil
2 tablespoons hot jalapeño jelly or 2 tablespoons honey
12 servings of 2 tablespoons each

Calories	133	Protein	.3 gm
Fat	13 gm	Carbohydrate	5 gm
Sodium	47 mg	Cholesterol	0

SALAD INGREDIENTS:

1 head of red leaf lettuce, washed and dried
2 oranges
1 grapefruit
1 ripe but firm avocado
6 large ripe but firm strawberries (optional)

1. Put all of the dressing ingredients in a food processor fitted with the metal blade and blend. I have tried adding only 1/2 cup of oil but the dressing is very thin in this case. By adding 2/3 cup oil, the dressing is thick and emulsified. The dressing is perfectly delicious without

31

the jalapeño jelly but the hot jelly does add a magical kick. Add it if you have it available. Refrigerate dressing in a glass jar. It will thicken with chilling. Makes 1 and 1/2 cups or 12 servings.

2. Cut off the tops and bottoms of oranges and grapefruit with a sharp knife and then peel from top to bottom, cutting away the white membranes completely. Slice the oranges. Cut the grapefruit slices into smaller quarters. Slice the avocado right before serving time so it does not turn brownish.

3. The dressing is higher in sugar and oil than any other dressing in this chapter but it is so flavorful just small amounts are sufficient. Arrange the torn lettuce in a large shallow dish and toss with half of the fruit and a couple of tablespoons of dressing. Arrange the rest of the fruit slices and avocado slices artistically around the salad and drizzle more dressing on top. Use 1/3 cup dressing total when tossing the salad and pass more at the table (in case someone wants to put it on his potatoes).
6 servings

Calories	230	Protein	2 gm
Fat	18 gm	Carbohydrate	18 gm
Sodium	54 mg	Cholesterol	0

Note: the original recipe is included in The Helen Corbitt Collection, edited by Elizabeth Ann Johnson, Houghton Mifflin, 1981.

RED CABBAGE AND APPLE SALAD
WITH POPPYSEED DRESSING

Here is another healthy way to use the poppyseed
  dressing.

3 cups thinly sliced and chopped red cabbage
2 Golden Delicious apples, peeled, cored, chopped
1/2 cup raisins
1/4 cup pecans, toasted and roughly chopped
3 tablespoons poppyseed dressing (recipe above)

1. Pour a couple of tablespoons of boiling water over the
raisins to plump or place in a small glass dish and
microwave the raisins on high power for 50 seconds.

2. After slicing and chopping the cabbage and apples,
toss with all of the ingredients. Kids love this salad when
it is slathered with twice the amount called for of the
poppyseed dressing. You can always keep their half of
the salad in a separate bowl with more dressing.
Serves 6 as a small separate salad or side dish.

Calories	148	Protein	1 gm
Fat	7 gm	Carbohydrate	22 gm
Sodium	21 mg	Cholesterol	0

NEW MEXICAN POTATO SALAD

This salad is New Mexican because I use my favorite Dixon chile powder and some ground New Mexican green chile - both obtained by mail from The Chile Shop in Santa Fe. It is much lower in fat than the usual mayonnaise-laden potato salad but high on spices and flavor, naturally attracting avid devotees.

2 pounds red-skinned potatoes, well-scrubbed
1 cup diced red bell pepper
1/2 cup diced green bell pepper
1 bunch green onions, chopped
1 can Mexicorn, 11 ounces
1/2 cup sliced black olives
1 tablespoon cilantro, snipped
2 tablespoons wine vinegar

SPICY DRESSING:

1 clove garlic, minced
1 teaspoon Dijon mustard
1/2 teaspoon salt
1/4 teaspoon ground cumin
2 tablespoons wine vinegar
3 tablespoons olive oil
2 teaspoons Dixon or red ground chile
1 teaspoon ground, dried green chile (optional)

1. Steam the potatoes for 30 minutes or until tender when pierced with a knife.

2. While potatoes are steaming, dice the rest of the vegetables and make the dressing.

3. When potatoes are cooked, drain them into a colander to cool for 5 minutes. Place the warm potatoes on a chopping board. Slice them and cut them into cubes. Place them into a bowl and douse with the wine vinegar and stir. When they are cooled down, add the dressing and stir in the peppers, green onions, corn kernels, olives and cilantro. Grind fresh pepper over the salad. Serves 6. A great salad for a barbecue.

Calories	259	Protein	5 gm
Fat	10 gm	Carbohydrate	40 gm
Sodium	496 mg	Cholesterol	0

LAYERED PESTO-CHEESE APPETIZER

This colorful appetizer is good with crackers, slices of French bread, or raw vegetables.

1 tablespoon olive oil
1/4 cup shallots
2 cups part-skim ricotta cheese (1 pound)
8 ounces light cream cheese
2 cloves garlic, minced through a press
6 ounces peeled red peppers from jar
2 teaspoons red chile powder
1/2 teaspon ground cumin

2 tablespoons canned jalapeño chiles, minced
Sliced black olives and minced cilantro for garnish

Cilantro Pesto

2 cups cilantro leaves
1/2 cup Asiago or Parmesan cheese, grated
1/3 cup toasted pumpkin seeds (pepitas)
2 cloves garlic
1 tablespoon lime juice
1/4 cup olive oil

1. Heat olive oil and saute the shallots until soft but not brown, for about 3 minutes.

2. Using a food processor beat the ricotta cheese and cream cheese until smooth. Blend in the sauteed shallots, garlic, the red peppers, cumin, and jalapeño chiles.

3. Remove the cheese mixture from the processor. Wipe out and add all the ingredients for the pesto. Blend well.

4. Rinse out the piece of cheesecloth in cold water and wring out. Use it to line a 6-cup mold. I use one of the white porcelain molds which has holes for drainage. You could even use a small clean terra cotta flower pot. Or just line a strainer with the cheesecloth. Use half of the red cheese mixture as the first layer. Place the pesto layer next. Finish with the rest of the cheese mixture as the last layer. Fold the ends of the cheesecloth over the top. Place your mold over a plate or if you are using a strainer, place over a bowl to catch the drips of whey from the

ricotta cheese. Refrigerate for several hours or overnight.

5. To unmold, fold back the cheesecloth. Place mold or
strainer upside down on the serving plate. Tap on
counter. Lift off mold and peel off the cheesecloth which
will leave a pretty texture on your appetizer. Garnish
with chopped cilantro and olives.
Serves 12 guests.

Calories	168	Protein	9 gm
Fat	13 gm	Carbohydrate	6 gm
Sodium	260 mg	Cholesterol	25 mg

SOPAS

CHAPTER II

THE SOUPS OF MEXICO

he soul of Mexican cuisine is the soup, drawing greatly on the country's Spanish heritage. Mexico even experienced a period of romantic inclination toward anything French, particularly during the rule of Porfirio Diaz. I have eaten creamed soups in small family restaurants which were French in their delicacy but they were made with Indian squash or the truffle-like huitlacoche.

Mexicans will make soup out of almost anything—roots, peelings, chicken feet, marrow bones, stomach lining (tripe), tomato skins, wild herbs.   Latin cuisine excels in stretching ingredients. Homemade caldo, or broth, provides the essence for all soups. Mexican cooks take a relaxed attitude toward caldo. You simply put a chicken or a meaty bone into a pot and simmer it with water and whatever else is available. My own Spanish-Californian grandmother merely flavored her soups, and many of her other dishes, with meat rather than using it as a main ingredient hence her infamous spaghetti sauce made with a few chicken wings. If you simmer your soup base for a long time, you can tenderize tough cuts of meat into succulent bites and you do not have to use a great deal of meat. For vegetables, you are cooking their essence into the broth rather than losing it in steam or throwing it out in cooking water. And soup is a wonderful medium to carry the jewels of unusual grains—barley, basmati rice, colorful beans, or cracked wheat. Many people who won't eat brown rice will happily eat it in soup. For me, soup is one of the most soul-satisfying parts of the meal. It is alleged that if you have a bowl of soup as a first course, you will have a sensation of being full and need to eat less of the rest of the meal.

DO NOT BE AFRAID OF STOCKS

For beginning cooks, making stock can elicit the same fear as making bread or puff pastry or deglazing pans. If they only knew. For about a decade in this country, there has been a mystifying gang, run amok, of Food Nazis, who have struck fear in the hearts of cooks. If you feel like using canned broth or a boullion cube, do it but do not look upon stock-making as a Herculean task. If all you want to do is make stock out of a chicken and some water, boiled for an hour. Do it. Forget the 3-hour stock rule. I never cook my chicken stock for 3 hours. Too much of a solid block of time to pay attention to the pot. Preferably I put a whole chicken, some water, and salt in my pressure cooker and simmer for about 50 minutes. I add celery, carrots, wine, and herbs if I have them. I do find it necessary to add some salt. Remember that the factory that makes canned broth isn't adding Chardonnay or leeks or fines herbes. The art of cooking has evolved into the overdoing of simply putting a pot on the fire.

Whenever I've collected enough bones or I find whole chickens on sale or I foresee the cooking of a recipe that will require stock, I make it. But I never let it rule my life. Sometimes all I have on hand is Swanson's reduced sodium canned broth (I prefer this one). I use it and the heavens do not wrathfully descend upon me.

EASY, FRIENDLY CHICKEN BROTH

1 whole chicken, 3 and 1/2 pounds
1/2 onion
1 carrot, peeled and cut in chunks
6 cloves garlic (yes, that is correct)
1 stalk celery with leaves, cut into chunks
1 tomato, cut in half
1/2 cup of dry white wine
8 cups water
1 sprig parsley
1 sprig thyme or 1 teaspoon dried thyme
1 teaspoon salt (optional)
1/4 teaspoon pepper

1. Wash off the chicken in cold water, remove packet of inner parts and discard or reserve for another use. Remove skin and cut off any excess pieces of chicken fat. Place chicken, breast-side up, in a pressure cooker or large pot. I use my faithful 8-quart pressure cooker (with built-in safety valve) and I never make stock the long way any more. Pour liquid over the top of the chicken, leaving the breast above the liquid to steam, and add chopped vegetables, herbs and salt. This is not a lot of salt for 8 and 1/2 cups of liquid. I feel that you need some salt to bring out the flavors of food, especially chicken broth, but if you are on a salt-free diet, please omit. Make this broth even if you only have half of the vegetables. It will still be good.

2. Bring the pressure cooker to a simmer and cook on low for 50 minutes. If you are using a regular pot, simmer for 1 and 1/2 hours. The pressure cooker extracts all the flavor from the chicken and I think that the white wine helps to draw nutrients from the chicken bones in the way that old cooks utilized vinegar. If you have a favorite herb like fresh oregano, dill, or sweet basil—use that in the broth. If you don't have any herbs, don't worry.

3. Allow your pressure cooker to cool down for at least 20 minutes. You can speed this up by placing the pot in the sink and running cold water over the lid. Once the pressure has dropped you will be able to safely remove the lid. New pressure cookers all have safety locks built in. Lift the chicken out and place on a dinner plate to cool. Put a wire strainer over a bowl and pour through the broth and vegetables. You can chill the broth so you can easily remove the fat on the surface or use one of those little pitchers that separates the fat from the liquid.

4. Use the steamed chicken breast for returning to the broth for chicken soup (see Janet's Doorstep Chicken Soup) or use for salads or sandwiches. Immediately eat the 2 little nuggets of meat on sides of the chicken back and invoke the spirit of James Beard who loved these among many other simple pleasures.
Makes about 2 quarts chicken broth

Calories	43	Protein	.6 gm
Fat	2 gm	Carbohydrate	6 gm
Sodium	4 mg	Cholesterol	0

REALLY EASY CHICKEN BROTH

About 1 quart canned chicken broth
  (reduced sodium)
1 quart water
1/4 cup white wine
1 chicken breast , skin removed, 1 pound
1/2 onion
2 cloves garlic
1 tomato with skin, cut in half
1 stalk celery with leaves, chopped
1 carrot, scraped, chopped
 Sprig of parsley and thyme

1. Place all the ingredients in a 2-quart pot and simmer for 25 minutes. Remove the chicken breast and simmer the broth without a lid for 10 minutes more. Strain into a large bowl. This broth can also be used for any of the soups requiring chicken stock as a base. It is not quite as chickeny as the previous recipe but it is very good. Best of all, this method is fast and takes just 30 minutes from the time you start whacking up the vegetables. You end up with both broth and nicely cooked chicken breast.

Makes about 2 quarts chicken broth

Calories	28	Protein	3 gm
Fat	,8 gm	Carbohydrate	2 gm
Sodium	36 mg	Cholesterol	4 mg

JANET BLANDINO REDMAN'S DOORSTEP CHICKEN SOUP

Whenever I suffer a cold or a winter flu, I long for the healing soups of my mother and grandmother and their way of enveloping their patients in such bustling care that they almost wished never to get well. I would curl up on the old brown chesterfield wrapped in a flannel blanket while the smells of chicken soup wafted into the room and waited impatiently for my tray. The tray would have the old Blue Willow bowl of chicken soup, soda crackers with a side dish of jelly, some tiny pieces of cut up fruit, a delicate piece of sponge cake, and a new movie magazine. Perfect fodder for an invalid of my standing; that is, I am rarely a sick person without an appetite.

When I was sick last February and made the trip into town to buy my poor self something to cook into soup, I returned to find a dented aluminum pot resembling Grandmama's, sitting on my doorstep with a reproachful note from Janet because I was not home in bed. The pot was filled to the brim with the most chickeny chicken soup. This soup, a gift from heaven, is one of the best I have ever savored. According to Janet, her Nicaraguan grandmother always added the lemon juice and brown rice to make it as healthful as possible.

1 whole chicken, 3 and 1/2 pounds, skinned
2 quarts water
1/2 onion
1 carrot, sliced
1 stalk celery with leaves, sliced
2 green onion, sliced
3 cloves garlic
2 sprigs of parsley
1 teaspoon cracked black pepper
1 teaspoon salt
Juice from 1 lemon

1. Place the chicken in a pressure cooker or stockpot, breastside up. I use my Fissler pressure cooker. Bring the chicken and rest of the ingredients to a simmer and begin the timing. The pressure cooker takes forty-five minutes and the regular stockpot takes one hour and fifteen minutes.

2. Remove chicken to a large plate and strain the broth into a bowl. Degrease the broth by pouring into one of those little pitchers which separates the fat from the liquid or chill for a couple of hours so that you can lift off the fat. Return the degreased broth to the pot and add the carrots, rice, and garlic. Simmer for 35 minutes to cook the rice sufficiently.

4 carrots, peeled and sliced
3/4 cup brown rice
2 cloves garlic, minced

1/2 cup minced green onions
2 cups shredded chicken
1-2 fresh jalapeño chiles, seeds and veins removed   and sliced
1/3 cup fresh lemon juice
1/4 cup cilantro, snipped with scissors

3. During the last 5 minutes of cooking, add the green onions, shredded chicken, chiles, lemon juice and cilantro. Spoon into wide soup bowls and eat immediately so as to repair your soul and cure all of your ills. It has been medically proven that chicken soup cures colds but when it is given the Hispanic touch with jalapeño chiles, we have the double whammy effect.

Serves 8 or 1 sick person for about a week.

Calories	188	Protein	14 gm
Fat	5 gm	Carbohydrate	21 gm
Sodium	375 mg	Cholesterol	31 mg

SOPA DE LIMA

It just so happens that one of the most celebrated dishes of the Mexican state of Yucatan is a soup—sopa de lima or lime soup which is really just a chicken soup lavishly flavored with the region's limas agrias (sour limes). I make it with California limes, rather unauthentic but delicious. Because of the pungency of the limes and the roasted garlic flavor, this soup more than any of the others transports me back to San Miguel de Allende, Guanajuato. This soup is Mexico.

2 quarts of chicken broth (see page 42)
1 and 1/2 chicken breasts, skinned, about 24 ounces
1 bay leaf
2 teaspoons oregano
1 teaspoon of oil
1 onion, chopped
1 and 1/2 cups green bell pepper, chopped
1 and 1/2 cups red bell pepper, chopped
1 mild Anaheim pepper, seeded and chopped
  (do not remove skin)
2 large tomatoes, roasted and finely chopped
6 cloves of garlic, roasted with husks
1/3 cup fresh lime juice
6 corn tortillas, cut into thin strips
4 limes, cut into wedges
1/4 cup cilantro, snipped with scissors
2 jalapeño chiles, seeds and veins removed and   chopped

1. Simmer the chicken breasts in the broth for 15 minutes and then skim off any foam on the surface, add the herbs and simmer for 15 more minutes. I have very successfully used 1 quart of water and 1 large can (49 ounces of Swanson's) chicken broth.

2. While the chicken is cooking, prepare the tortillas by squeezing 1 lime over the surface and baking the strips in a preheated 350 degree oven for about 10 minutes or until golden and crisp. By oven-crisping the tortillas you are omitting the usual technique of frying the tortilla strips thereby removing a few grams of fat!

3. Remove the chicken and cool while you prepare the rest of the soup.

4. In the teaspoon of oil, saute the onion, bell peppers, and the chopped Anaheim chile. Roast the tomatoes and garlic in a dry skillet for about 10 minutes. Remove the tomato skins and chop with 4 cloves of garlic.
Add to the saute pan with the onions and peppers and simmer together for 5 minutes and then stir all of this mixture into the chicken broth. Shred the chicken breast with your fingers and add to the broth along with lime juice. Heat to a gentle simmer.

5. Prepare little bowls to hold the condiments: the lime wedges, the cilantro, and combine the chopped jalapeños, the juice from 2 lime wedges and 2 minced cloves of roasted garlic   Ladle soup into bowls and sprinkle with the crisp tortilla strips. Each person can add more lime juice, cilantro, or chopped jalapeño-garlic mixture.
8 servings

Calories	232	Protein	23 gm
Fat	5 gm	Carbohydrate	26 gm
Sodium	105 mg	Cholesterol	49 mg

MEXICAN MINESTRONE
WITH CILANTRO PESTO

After the heat of Indian summer, I can barely wait each year for the first cold night of autumn, that first shock of darkness coming at five o'clock. Then I can make my *a la cinco de la tarde* soup which brings gladness to my kitchen.

With its profusion of beans, spinach pasta, and vegetables this soup will make you feel healthy. It has
become a favorite in our family and for an informal
gathering it is greatly appreciated along with bread and
wine.

1 cup pinto beans
1 cup black beans
6 cups water
1 tablespoon olive oil
2 onions, chopped
2 red bell peppers, chopped
2 cloves garlic, minced
2 leeks, well-rinsed and chopped
2 quarts of chicken stock
2 cups crushed, canned tomatoes
1 sprig fresh rosemary or 1 teaspoon dried rosemary
1 teaspoon salt (optional)
1 to 2 teaspoons ground chile (like Dixon)
2 teaspoon oregano
3 zucchini, sliced
6 carrots, peeled and sliced
2 cups kale, chopped
1 cup cabbage, chopped
1 and 1/2 cups spinach or semolina macaroni

1. If you are in a hurry you could begin the recipe by
substituting canned beans but it is best to drain them in
a sieve and rinse away the salty residue under cold

running water. Or to start from scratch, wash your dried beans under running water and remove any stones. Place them in a large pot and add water about 2 inches over the level of the beans. Bring to a boil, simmering briskly for 3 minutes. Turn off the heat and allow the beans to steep for at least 2 hours. Then pour off all of this simmering liquid and add 6 cups of fresh water. Bring to a boil and simmer until the beans are tender, about 1 hour and 30 minutes.

2. Meanwhile, saute the onions, peppers, garlic, and leeks in the olive oil. You could reduce the amount of olive oil required to just 1 teaspoon if you are really watching fats. Just remember that when you are using a small amount of oil for sauteeing, vegetables tend to stick and burn more easily. Use a nonstick pan and keep stirring. After the beans have simmered for 45 minutes, add the sauteed vegetable mixture. When the beans are tender, add the salt and other seasonings. Next add the chicken stock, the crushed tomatoes, and the chopped vegetables. Simmer for 10 minutes and then stir in the macaroni. Simmer for another 10 minutes or until the macaroni is tender.

3. Serve in wide soup bowls and let each guest add a tablespoon of cilantro pesto. Some pesto addicts spread the pesto on bread instead of butter. The minestrone is also wonderful without the pesto.

Serves 8

Calories	358	Protein	16 gm
Fat	5 gm	Carbohydrate	65 gm
Sodium	150 mg	Cholesterol	0

CILANTRO PESTO

This is one of those instances where the taste of the cilantro becomes milder rather than stronger and in this case, rather than the 1/2 cup of oil required for traditional pesto, we are using 2 tablespoons. You can also use this pesto to toss with pasta or as spread on bread.

2 tablespoons olive oil
1/4 cup freshly grated Parmesan or Asiago cheese
2 cloves garlic
1 cup cilantro
1 teaspoon dried mild oregano
Juice from 1/2 lime

1. Place all of the above ingredients into the bowl of a food processor and blend into a rough texture. Store in refrigerator. Makes 3/4 cup pesto or 12 servings

Calories	31	Protein	9 gm
Fat	3 gm	Carbohydrate	.4 gm
Sodium	38 mg	Cholesterol	2 mg

FAVORITE PESTO APPETIZER

Cut thin slices from a loaf of French or sourdough bread and spread a thin layer of cilantro pesto (or basil pesto) over the tops. Then lay over the tops, a strip of roasted red pepper (the kind you buy in a glass jar in Italian stores or roast your own). Broil or toast the bread slices under a broiler or in a toaster oven just until the pesto is bubbly, roughly a minute. Watch carefully.

SOPA DE FIDEOS
ANGEL HAIR PASTA SOUP

The healthy aspect of Mexican cooking is happily linked to an abundance of carbohydrates in the form of tortillas, beans, rice and pasta. Mexican cooks probably use more fideos than any other pasta, the best being the tiniest, wirelike loops. The closest thing to fideos is angel hair pasta. You can search out Mexican grocery stores or order fideos from Pendery's of Fort Worth, Texas. See RESOURCES.

A dominant and unique aspect of true Mexican cooking is the custom of toasting ingredients. In particular, rice and fideos are frequently toasted in oil as a first step thus adding flavor but more fat. I have found that the flavor can be retained by toasting the fideos in the oven minus the oil.

12 ounces of Mexican fideos or vermicelli
1 cup chopped onion
2 cups peeled, seeded tomatoes
  (you can substitute canned plum tomatoes)
1 teaspoon minced garlic
2 quarts chicken stock (reduced sodium)
1 mild fresh green chile (Anaheim), chopped, seeded
1 teaspoon mild ground chile
  (like Dixon or California)
1/4 cup grated Asiago or Parmesan cheese

1. Grind the tomatoes, onion, and garlic together in a food processor or chop by hand. Stir into the chicken stock. Bring to a simmer. Add the chopped green chile and the chile powder. Simmer for 15 minutes to blend flavors.

2. Break up the coils of fideos on a jelly roll pan and toast for about 8 to 10 minutes in a preheated 350 degree oven. Add the toasted fideos to the soup and simmer for 3 to 4 minutes. After ladling the soup into bowls, sprinkle tops with Parmesan cheese. I usually serve this soup with a warm tomato salsa that each person can stir into his soup for a more picante flavoring.
8 servings

Calories	233	Protein	8 gm
Fat	3 gm	Carbohydrate	42 gm
Sodium	71 mg	Cholesterol	2 mg

ME AND HUGO'S
CALDO DE TLALPEÑO

Have you ever eaten something in a restaurant and you knew the moment of the second mouthful that you had to have the recipe? In the course of writing four cook-books I have found that most chefs are protective of their recipes but they love to talk food. For concocting a soup, you don't need a recipe but knowing a rough assemblage of ingredients helps. Each time I tasted Hugo's (in Van Nuys, California) Caldo de Tlalpeño, it was one of the best soups I had eaten in or out of Mexico. Hugo evaded all of my dumb questions with smart, dumb answers. Forgive me Hugo but you challenged me and I went after your soup. It was the ground, dried chipotle chile that held me up for awhile because Hugo denied its existence.

Do not expect this soup to be a fifteen minute foray into the kitchen but it is not difficult . Besides it will be the equivalent of drinking 10 hot multivitamins.

1 whole chicken, about 3 and 1/2 pounds,
 skin removed
3 quarts of cold water
2 stalks of celery with leaves, cut into large pieces
4 cloves garlic
1 onion, halved
2 teaspoons oregano
1 and 1/2 chicken breasts, 24 ounces, skinned
1 pound red-skinned potatoes, halved
2 green bell peppers, cored and cut into chunks
2 stalks celery with leaves, sliced thickly
1 tomato, roasted under broiler, ground in blender
2 teaspoons mild ground chile
 (like California or pasilla)
1 to 2 teaspoons ground, dried chipotle chile
1/2 cup green onion, chopped
2 cups fresh spinach, washed, stemmed, shredded
1/4 cup cilantro
1 ripe but firm avocado, skinned and sliced
Yellow Rice, stirred into soup at table

1. Rinse off chicken and cover with cold water in a 5 to 6 quart pot. Bring to a simmer and skim off the foam as it comes to the surface during the first 15 minutes of cooking. Next add the celery, garlic, onion, and oregano. Simmer for 1 hour. Add the chicken breasts and cook for 25 more minutes. Remove the breasts and strain the stock. Remove any fat by chilling or using a pitcher that separates the fat from the liquid.

2. Put the stock back into the pot and simmer with the potatoes, bell peppers, celery, pureed tomato, and chile powders. Cook the vegetables and stock for 25 minutes.

3. Meanwhile, prepare the Yellow Rice and chop the green onions, spinach, cilantro, and slice the avocado at the last moment, squeezing some lime or lemon juice over the slices to keep from turning brown. Shred the cooled chicken breasts.

4. A few minutes before serving time, stir the green onions, shredded spinach, cilantro, shredded chicken breast, and avocado cubes into the soup. When you order Hugo's soup at his restaurant, you can hear him chopping all this stuff back in the kitchen. He adds it at the last minute just before it is brought to you. At the table, pass the Yellow Rice for each person to add to his soup bowl.

8 servings

Calories	258	Protein	23 gm
Fat	8 gm	Carbohydrate	23 gm
Sodium	99 mg	Cholesterol	49 mg

YELLOW RICE

2 cups boiling water
1 cup long-grain white rice
2 teaspoons butter or margarine
1/2 teaspoon salt (Hugo uses more)
1 teaspoon tumeric powder

1. Add the rice and the rest of the ingredients to the simmering water. minutes longer. Turn heat to low and keep rice cooking gently for 30 minutes. Do not peek. Turn off heat and still do not remove lid for 10 minutes. The rice will continue to steam into fluffiness. Place in a bowl, fluffing the rice with a fork and let each person add a dollop of rice to his Caldo de Tlapeño and offer a blessing for Hugo's stubbornness and good soup.

Note: I buy dried whole chipotles from the Green Chile Fix Company and they ship them from Santa Fe. See Resources. I then grind them into a powder using an old electric coffee grinder that I have reserved just for chiles, dried garlic, and spices.

8 servings

Calories	94	Protein	2 gm
Fat	1 mg	Carbohydrate	19 gm
Sodium	147 mg	Cholesterol	2 mg

Note: you could use a long-grain brown rice but you must use 2 and 1/2 cups water for cooking and simmer the rice on low for about 40 minutes. Allow rice to steam off the heat for another 10 minutes without removing the lid. This ingredient is not included in the nutritional analysis above.

ENCHILADA SOUP

A soup with a reminicense of enchiladas. The young bachelor down the street was a tester and he immediately begged for the recipe. He makes it in a crock pot and eats it all week for sustenance before the weekend.

1/2 cup pinto beans
1/2 cup red beans or black beans
8 cups water
4 cloves garlic
2 onions, chopped
6 dried California or New Mexican chiles
2 corn tortillas, torn into small pieces
4 tomatoes, skins removed and chopped
   (2 and 1/2 cups)
1 can tomato paste (6 ounces)
1 teaspoon ground cumin
2 teaspoons oregano
1 tablespoon ground chile powder
   (like Dixon or California)
1 teaspoon Tabasco
1 can black olives, sliced
1/4 pound reduced-fat Cheddar cheese, grated
2 tablespoon chives or chopped green onions
Salt to taste
3 corn tortillas cut into strips for homemade chips

1. Rinse beans and pick over for stones. Put in large pot and cover with water. Bring to a boil and simmer for 3 minutes. Turn off heat and soak beans for 1 hour. Pour off soaking water and add 8 cups of fresh water to the

beans along with the chopped onion and garlic. Simmer for 1 hour or until beans are tender yet firm. After the presoaking, you can do this step in a crock pot but cook the beans and onions for 5 hours instead of 1 hour. Now add the rest of the ingredients.

2. While the beans are cooking wash off the dried chiles in cold water. Break apart and remove the large veins and seeds. Place the chiles in a 2-quart saucepan and cover with water. Simmer for 15 minutes. Remove and place in a blender with a cup of fresh water. Blend until pureed and then add the pieces of corn tortilla and tomatoes. Grind together. Add the to the beans along with the tomato paste and spices. Simmer for 45 minutes. During the last 15 minutes, stir in the sliced black olives.

3. To crisp the tortilla strips so that they are fat-free, toast them on a baking sheet in a preheated 350 degree oven for about 10 minutes or until crisp and golden but not browned. If you are not concerned about low-fat tortilla strips or you are a bachelor , just crumble a good brand of store-bought, unsalted tortilla strips for your soup.

4. Taste for salt, adding from 1/2 teaspoon to 1 and 1/2 teaspoons. These amounts are optional and are not included in the nutritional analysis.

4. To serve: ladle the Enchilada Soup over a few crisp tortilla strips placed in each bowl and sprinkle with some of the shredded cheese and chives. This is a very hearty and filling soup and you only need cold beer and some

warm bolillos or tortillas to accompany it. If I have a
couple of cups of this soup left I freeze it and then when
I have leftover vegetable soup, I combine the two soups.
If soup is too thick after refrigeration, thin it with
reduced sodium chicken broth.
Serves 8

Calories	246	Protein	12 gm
Fat	8 gm	Carbohydrate	32 gm
Sodium	428 gm	Cholesterol	10 mg

SPICY SPLIT PEA SOUP

My husband thinks this is the best recipe for split pea that
I've ever made, probably because I have indoctrinated
him into believing that nothing is good without chile.

1 pound of split peas
8 cups water
2 cups chopped white onion
1 bay leaf
2 stalks celery with leaves, diced (1 cup)
*The white part of 2 leeks, well-washed and diced
    (1 cup)*
1 yam, peeled and diced
3 cloves garlic, minced
1 tablespoon fresh thyme
1 teaspoon oregano
2 teaspoons ground chile
1/2 teaspoon cumin powder
1/4 teaspoon cinnamon
2 carrots, peeled and diced (1 cup)
1 ten-ounce package of frozen petite peas
Lowfat milk, 1 cup for thinning soup

1. Rinse the dried peas and then place in a 3-quart pot. Cover with water and add everything but the carrots and frozen peas. Simmer the soup for about 1 and a half to 2 hours.

2. You can puree the soup CAREFULLY in a blender only doing 2 cups at a time. Or you can use a food mill or a hand blender, a marvelous tool that you can plunge right into the cooking pot and puree the soup without pouring hot liquids back and forth.

3. After pureeing the soup I add the diced carrots and the baby peas. Simmer the soup and newly added vegetables for about 15 minutes or until the carrots are tender. If the soup seems too thick, before serving thin it with the milk, a small amount at a time.

8 servings

Calories	291	Protein	18 gm
Fat	2 gm	Carbohydrate	53 gm
Sodium	105mg	Cholesterol	2 mg

SWEET POTATO AND JALAPEÑO SOUP

Momentarily I have been led astray from authentic soups. This soup is served at one of those very California restaurants along the coast and I loved it at my first mouthful. The original recipe uses a lot of heavy cream so I have worked hard at this recipe to reduce the cream and yet fool our mouths.

1 and 1/2 pounds sweet potatoes, peeled and diced
4 carrots, peeled and diced
6 cups chicken broth
1 teaspoon fresh thyme
2 teaspoons oil
1 cup chopped onion
2 jalapeño chiles, seeded and minced
2 teaspoons maple syrup
Pinch of cayenne pepper
12 ounces lowfat evaporated milk (2%)

1. Simmer the sweet potatoes, carrots, and the fresh thyme in the chicken broth for 45 minutes. Puree the sweet potato, 3 carrots, and broth together in a food processor.

2. In 2 teaspoons of oil saute the onion and chiles over very low heat, stirring frequently so they do not brown. Stir the sauteed vegetables into the sweet potato puree. Add the remaining diced carrot, maple syrup, cayenne pepper, and the milk. Blend with a whisk. You can also use nonfat milk (not as rich tasting). Here the restaurant adds a cup to 1 and 1/2 cups of heavy cream. Heat gently and serve in small bowls as a first course. If you could allow yourself the splurge, whisk in 1/4 cup of heavy cream just as you were finishing the soup. This amount of cream adds 2.75 grams of fat or 25 calories to each serving.

8 servings

Calories	175	Protein	5 gm
Fat	4 gm	Carbohydrate	30 gm
Sodium	73 mg	Cholesterol	8 mg

TOASTED SOPA DE TORTILLA

In my *Red and Green Chile Book* there is a recipe for tortilla soup which is full of vegetables and worth a whole dinner's appetite but this one is very close to a soup I had in the town of Patzcuaro where we had gone for a restful holiday. We went back to the same restaurant on the square to eat Toasted Sopa de Tortilla every day.

Often in Mexico, the purer versions of tortilla soup have no vegetables but only crisp tortilla strips and some shreds of chicken floating in a chile broth. But typical of the Mexican kitchen, the ingredients are toasted to heighten the flavors.

6 ancho chiles
6 pasilla chiles
5 unpeeled cloves of garlic
1 onion
4 tomatoes
1 can tomato paste (6 ounces)
2 quarts chicken broth (reduced sodium broth)
1 whole chicken breast, 1 pound, skinned simmered in
*   the above broth*
10 corn tortillas, cut into tiny strips
2 avocados, ripe but firm
Mexican fresh white cheese like queso fresco or
*   Jack cheese, 1 cup (reduced-fat cheese)*

1. Using a cast-iron pan, toast the chiles over medium heat until they soften and give off a toasty aroma. DO NOT DARKEN the chiles, just toast them. It takes about

2 minutes. Next place in the pan, the unpeeled garlic cloves and the unpeeled onion. Over medium heat, toast them until they soften, taking about 20 minutes during which time you can take care of the chiles.

2. Break the chiles apart and cover with boiling water. Steep for 1 hour. Now the easy part. Place the chiles in a blender with 1/2 cup water at a time and puree in batches, adding a little of the onion and garlic. Char the tomatoes over a flame or under a broiler. Remove the skins and puree them with the last batch of chiles. In a large pot, combine the chile-tomato puree, tomato paste, and 1 and 1/2 quarts chicken broth. Simmer together for 30 minutes. Meanwhile, poach the chicken breast in 2 cups of the reserved chicken broth for 25 minutes. Remove the chicken to cool on a plate and strain the broth into the pot containing the chile puree. When you can handle the chicken, remove from bones and shred. Add to soup.

3. Bake the tortilla strips on a baking sheet in a preheated 350 degree oven for about 10 minutes or until golden and crisp.

4. When serving the tortilla soup, pour into bowls and garnish around the edges with the crisp tortilla strips. Place avocado slices on the top. Pass the cheese for each person to add to his bowl.

Serves 8

Calories	388	Protein	24 gm
Fat	16 gm	Carbohydrate	41 gm
Sodium	379 mg	Cholesterol	43mg

MEXICAN VEGETABLE SALSA SOUP

I fix this soup when I have lived too well and just want vegetables. Perfect meal for a rich peasant with a fine loaf and a robust bottle.

10 cups liquid (water, stock, vegetable water)
1 cup tomato salsa, storebought or homemade
2 stalks celery with leaves, sliced
1/2 onion, chopped
2 cloves garlic, minced
1 teaspoon oregano
1 teaspoon sweet basil
4 carrots, sliced
Choose 3 of any of the following vegetables:
1 cup green beans
1 cup sliced zucchini
1 cup corn kernels, fresh or frozen
1 cup of cubed red potatoes (or Russet)
1/2 cup frozen peas
1 cup of chayote, peeled and diced
1/2 cup rosamarinas (rice-shaped pasta) or macaroni

1. Combine all of the liquid, the salsa, and the vegetables of your choice. Simmer for 15 minutes.

2. Then stir in the rosamarinas or macaroni and simmer for 10 more minutes.

8 servings

Calories	105	Protein	4 gm
Fat	.6 gm	Carbohydrate	22 gm
Sodium	74 mg	Cholesterol	0

Note: Since I concoct a lot of soups and freeze leftovers, one day I successfully combined leftover Mexican Vegetable Salsa Soup with Enchilada Soup So now I try to have both soups in the freezer.

Also the Mexican Vegetable Salsa Soup done with corn, zucchini, and green beans is a good base for that old standby Sopa de Albondigas. See recipe below for Albondigas which are just small meatballs and add them to the vegetable soup. Also delete the pasta if you are doing the meatball soup.

ALBONDIGAS FOR ALBONDIGAS SOUP

Often meatball soup is the only soup served in Mexican restaurants and it is often salty. You can make it so much better at home.

1/2 pound very lean ground beef (15%)
1/2 pound ground turkey (7% fat)
1/4 cup dry bread crumbs
1/4 cup cornmeal
1/4 cup finely chopped onion
3 canned green chiles, chopped finely
1 clove garlic, minced through a press
2 tablespoons fresh mint, minced
1/2 cup parsley, minced
1/2 teaspoon ground cumin
1/2 teaspoon salt

1. Mix all of the ingredients together in a large bowl and form into small meatballs about the size of a walnut. Drop them into simmering soup (see recipe above) and cook over low heat with the lid on the pot for 20 minutes.

2. Then add the vegetables, like zucchini, carrots, and green beans, which have been cut into small pieces. Simmer the soup for another 15 minutes.
Serves 8. Makes 16 meatballs, 2 per person.

Calories	140	Protein	11 gm
Fat	7 gm	Carbohydrate	7 gm
Sodium	241 mg	Cholesterol	40 mg

TARASCAN BEAN SOUP

From the state of Michoacan, here is one of the most delicate of Mexican soups. Because of the rich taste of pinto beans, it is unnecessary to add more than the small amount of olive oil for sauteeing the vegetables. By completely pureeing the beans, the smoothness of the soup maximizes the gentle flavors. When I was testing this recipe, I first did the soup by only pureeing enough beans to thicken the broth. But for the second test I pureed everything. What a marvelous difference it made and my husband thought that I had added another ingredient. A sister to this soup is a regular every Saturday at the famous El Mirador in San Antonio, Texas.

12 ounces pinto beans
6 cups water
2 ancho chiles
1 onion, chopped roughly
3 cloves garlic, minced

---

4 tomatoes, broiled
1 onion with skins on, cut in half
4 cloves garlic
1 tablespoon olive oil
1 teaspoon ground cumin
1 teaspoon oregano
3 cups chicken broth (reduced sodium)
2 ancho chiles
4 corn tortillas, cut into strips

1. Rinse the beans in a sieve, picking through them for stones. Place in a large pot and cover with water. Bring to a simmer, cook for 3 minutes, and then allow the beans to stand in the liquid for at least 3 hours. Drain off this soaking water and discard.

2. Add 6 cups of fresh water to the drained beans along with the onion, garlic and ancho chiles which have been broken into pieces. I like to use my pressure cooker for beans because it shortens the time needed for cooking. If using a pressure cooker, put on the lid and bring up to a simmer (for the proper pressure) and cook for 45 minutes. If you are using a regular pot, simmer the beans for about 1 and 1/2 hours or until tender.

3. Meanwhile, prepare the rest of the soup. Place the tomatoes, onion, and garlic in a pie pan and broil just until the tomato skins blister and brown. Turn the tomatoes over once. This should take about 5 minutes total. When cool enough to handle, skin the tomatoes and squeeze out the seeds. Remove the skins from the onion and garlic. Place everything in a food processor and puree roughly. Don't clean out the processor because you will be using it to puree the beans. Heat the oil simmer the tomato puree for 10 minutes, adding the spices.

4. When the beans have been cooked, cool them down a little before attempting to puree them along with the cooked ancho chiles in the food processor. Puree them in 3 cup batches. As you work, pour the puree into the pot with the tomato-onion mixture. Stir the chicken broth into the mixture and simmer for 15 minutes. Watch since purees burn easily. Taste for salt and add 1/2 teaspoon to 1 and 1/2 teaspoons. This amount is not included in the nutritional analysis.

5. Toast the tortilla strips for 8 minutes in a preheated 350 degree oven.
They should be crisp but not browned.

6. Toast the ancho chile in a dry skillet being careful not to burn it. Chop or crumble the chile and serve it sprinkled over the top of each serving of soup along with the homemade tortilla chips. The taste of the ancho chile has been compared to that of a spicy raisin. Pendery's of

Texas (see Resources) has great ancho chiles. I have been stuck with many dusty, hard ancho chiles but Pendery's really does have wonderfully soft and sweet anchos which do resemble big raisins.

8 servings

Calories	230	Protein	12 gm
Fat	3 gm	Carbohydrate	40 gm
Sodium	303 mg	Cholesterol	0

BLACK BEAN SOUP WITH MARINATED RICE

Black beans, very popular in the Carribean, the Yucatan, and Cuba, seem to be found in everything from chips to salads and chile. From the very first time I sampled black bean soup in Merida, Yucatan I was hooked. I have played with this recipe a great deal in my own kitchen, adding and deleting ingredients such as celery and bell peppers, finally settling on this one as my very favorite.

1 pound black beans
1 ham bone or 4 ounces of lean ham (96% fat free)
2 quarts of water
1 onion, half
3 cloves garlic

• • • • • • • • •

3 cloves garlic
1 onion, peeled and quartered
2 cups chicken broth (reduced-sodium broth)
1 chipotle chile en adobo from can
1/2 teaspoon salt

Marinated rice:

1 and 1/2 cups cooked rice
1/3 cup minced onion
1 tablespoon olive oil
3 tablespoons vinegar
1/2 teaspoon freshly ground black pepper

1. If you want the beans to remain wonderfully pitch black, you cannot presoak them with the hot water method. Just put the beans in a sieve and rinse them off. Place in a pot, cover with 8 cups of water, the onion, the garlic, and the ham bone. Bring to a boil, turn down the heat to low, and simmer for about 1 and 1/2 hours. The ham will add some salt so taste the beans before you add more salt.

2. While the beans are cooking, place the onion pieces in a small pie pan with the garlic, 1 cup of the chicken broth, and the chipotle chile. Cover with foil and bake at 350 degrees for 30 minutes. Set aside. Meanwhile toss together the ingredients for the marinated rice so that the flavors may blend.

3. Puree the beans and the onion-broth mixture in batches in a food processor, adding the remaining chicken broth. Leave some of the beans whole for more texture. If the soup is too thick, thin with chicken broth using about 1/4 cup at a time until the soup is of the desired consistency. This velvety soup is topped with a table-spoon of marinated rice for each serving. You may also pass lime wedges, sherry, or bottled hot sauce to be

added at the table. Also delicious as a topping are a couple of rings of the Pink Pickled Onions, page10.
8 servings

Calories	301	Protein	17 gm
Fat	4 gm	Carbohydrate	51 gm
Sodium	372 mg	Cholesterol	7 mg

EASY MEXICAN GAZPACHO

I have combined the gazpacho recipe from my *California Rancho Cooking* and made it easier, spicier, and with less of my beloved olive oil which was used in great abundance on our rancho. Olive oil is still fat, although healthier than most I have found that when I want to use olive oil for seasoning rather than sauteeing, I can use less oil if I use a very flavorful one.

2 cloves garlic
1/2 red onion or mild onion (about 1 cup)
1 cucumber, peeled
1/4 cup of roasted and peeled Italian red peppers
  from jar
Juice from 1 lemon
2 tablespoons red wine vinegar
1 can Italian plum tomatoes, drained
1/2 teaspoon hot pepper sauce
1 tablespoon virgin olive oil
1/2 teaspoon freshly ground pepper
1/2 teaspoon salt
1 tablespoon fresh sweet basil or
1/2 teaspoon dried basil

1/2 teaspoon dried basil
3 tablespoon cilantro, snipped with scissors
1 cup regular tomato juice
4 cups spicy tomato juice

Gazpacho Vegetables

1 cucumber, peeled and diced or use English cucumber, unpeeled
4 green onion, minced
2 fresh tomatoes, diced

1. Plan to make the gazpacho at least two hours before you need it so the flavors may season. In a blender, place all the ingredients for the gazpacho with 1 cup of the spicy tomato juice. Withhold the diced gazpacho vegetables for stirring in later. Blend the gazpacho until ingredients are well-mixed and pureed with some texture remaining. Pour into a 2-quart glass bowl and add the rest of the spicy tomato juice and the diced cucumber, green onions, and tomatoes.
Serves 8

Calories	87	Protein	3 gm
Fat	2 gm	Carbohydrate	17 gm
Sodium	864 mg	Cholesterol	0

SOPA DE MAIZ

Corn soup is just one of the ways in which a native ingredient such as maize is treated very delicately. When this is made in Mexico, the thick crema doble is stirred into the soup to finish it off. In our version the pureed vegetables help fool our palates.

2 packages (1 pound each) frozen sweet
   corn kernels or 6 cups fresh corn kernels
2 teaspoons butter or olive oil
1 cup chopped onion
2 cups potatoes, cubed (1 and 1/4 pounds)
3 cups chicken stock (reduced sodium or homemade)
1 red bell pepper
1 cup low-fat milk
2 teaspoons sugar
1/2 teaspoon salt
2 tablespoons roasted green chile
   (Anaheim, poblano, or New Mexican)
1 teaspoon butter
2 fresh jalapeño chiles, sliced in rings

1. Simmer the corn kernels and the potatoes in the chicken stock for 15 minutes.

2. Meanwhile saute-steam the onion in the butter, using a saute pan and pressing a piece of waxed paper over the top of the pan. Press around the edges and the wax paper will adhere and keep in the good juices. Saute the onion for 8 minutes or until soft. Add the onion to the corn and potatoes.

3. Run the corn, potato, and onion mixture through the medium disk of a food mill and then place the puree back in the pot you used for simmering and add the milk.

4. Roast the red pepper and the green chile pepper under a boiler until blackened. Remove skins and chop the peppers. Add to the corn soup. Simmer the soup for 10 minutes, stirring frequently so it doesn't stick as purees are prone to do. Quick-saute the jalapeño rings. Over each serving of soup, float a couple of jalapeño rings on the top.

8 servings

Calories	182	Protein	7 gm
Fat	3 gm	Carbohydrate	36 gm
Sodium	439 mg	Cholesterol	6 mg

MEXICAN SEAFOOD

CHAPTER III

MEXICAN SEAFOOD DISHES

n the coastal cities and villages of Mexico, seafood is treated with great respect and fondness. Some of our most memorable fish recipes were those prepared by fishermen on whose boat we spent the day, particularly on the small boats you can rent, crew intact, off the small island, Isla de Mujeres, just a few miles from the Yucatan Peninsula. There, they barbecue fish over palmetto twigs rather than the chunks of mesquite used in other parts of Mexico.

When barbecuing or grilling fish, never place the fish over a fiercely hot barbecue. When our captain-fisherman-cook barbecued a butterflied mero (sea bass) on the beach, the palmetto coals, covered with a white ash, were smoldering so gently I thought the fire was dead until I held my hand over it.

Along the beach in Mexico, you can quickly fashion a grill out of green sticks but back in your own backyard, the best fish grill is one of those stainless steel hinged grills that you find in hardware stores or chain drugstores. The price is usually under $10. These grills are perfect for filets and butterflied fish because you can turn the fish without stabbing at it with a spatula. Before placing the fish inside, oil the grill or spray it with Pam.

Lastly, when barbecuing or grilling fish, be overzealous about watching it. Stand by the fire, with a cooling libation, watching. When my husband barbecues anything, he puts the meat over the fire and then leaves to paint the garage, returning to find a relic only suitable for Carbon 14 dating. If you've ever known an avid barbecuer or asador, as they were known on the ranchos of California, they nurse their fires, their wood, their marinades, their meats, their glasses of wine until they have created theater around the barbecue itself. Anything outside of that is immaterial.

GRILLED YUCATAN FISH

In Yucatan, sea bass is often rubbed with a marinade of sour orange juice, lime juice, oil, and achiote paste but I have substituted the paste with a canned chipotle chile en adobo. The canned chipotle is easy to find in Mexican grocery stores and in the ethnic section of some super-markets. Although the chipotle is just a smoked jalapeño chile, it is hotter and adds a mysterious flavor that most people can never guess.

1 and 1/2 pounds sea bass, rock cod, or red snapper filets
1/4 cup lime juice
1/2 cup orange juice
1 teaspoon grated orange peel
1 tablespoon olive oil
1 teaspoon minced garlic
1 chipotle en adobo from can
1 tablespoon adobo juice from can
1/4 cup minced cilantro

1.   Simmer the lime juice, orange juice, peel, olive oil, garlic, chipotle, and adobo juice for 15 minutes until reduced and concentrated. Stir in the cilantro. Cool the marinade and then pour over fish. Let them stand for 30 minutes before cooking.

2.   Broil or grill over a barbecue for 3 to 5 minutes per side depending upon the thickness of the filets. Stick a fork into the middle of the filet and if it pulls away easily,

almost flaking, the fish is done. I have used this same marinade over whole, cleaned squid and then grilled them on an oiled barbecue for about 2 minutes per side. Sliced them into rings they make a great appetizer while you are standing by the barbecue.

Serves 6.

Calories	128	Protein	18 gm
Fat	4 gm	Carbohydrate	4 gm
Sodium	139 mg	Cholesterol	39 mg

BAJA CALIFORNIA FISH TACOS

In many of the seaport villages of Mexican, there are innumerable variations on the theme of fish tacos. Sometimes the fish is battered and deep-fried, sometimes it is boiled and flaked or my favorite, grilled over a brazier of smoky mesquite. The cook will offer you a variety of condiments that also vary from sliced radishes and lettuce to thinly cut white cabbage.

Even if you are not going to make tacos, this is a great marinade for brushing on fish and is particularly good if you are barbecuing. The same marinade works well on chicken.

1 and 1/2 pounds red snapper, rock cod, or shark filets
1/4 cup lime juice
1 tablespoon olive oil
1 teaspoon minced garlic
1 chipotle chile en adobo from can or 1 teaspoon
  chile powder
1/2 cup chopped onion

1/4 cup snipped cilantro
2 cups of chopped iceberg or romaine lettuce
Salsa, use good bottled or make recipe below
12 fresh corn tortillas

1. Blend together the lime juice, olive oil, garlic, and chipotle chile. Add a little juice from the chipotle can if you want extra flavor. Rub this mixture all over the fish filets. Allow them to marinate for at least 20 minutes at room temperature before cooking.

2. Broil the fish filets 6 inches under a hot broiler for 3 minutes and then turn over. Broil about 3 to 4 minutes. The exact timing will depend upon the thickness of the filets so it is best to check after 3 minutes. When a fork is stuck into the filet, the fish should barely flake. You want it to remain moist.

3. Remove the filets from the broiler and onto a plate where you may cut them into smaller pieces. For the taco filling add chopped onion and cilantro to the fish. Warm the corn tortillas by wrapping them in foil and placing them in a preheated 350 degree oven for about 10 minutes or heat them on a comal or griddle as I do. Wrap the warm tortillas in a tea towel.

4. Everyone spoons some of the fish-cilantro mixture into a soft tortilla and adds salsa and lettuce.
Serves 6

Calories	296	Protein	24 gm
Fat	6 gm	Carbohydrate	29 gm
Sodium	236 mg	Cholesterol	35 mg

LUCY'S HOT SALSA

In October we drive to the Tehachapi mountains for fresh apples and an early breakfast at a little diner frequented by only the local folk. For the diner a Mexican lady makes this salsa and it is kept on each table in one of the plastic squeeze bottles, looking sort of lethal green (because she adds more jalapeños) but superb on omelets.

1 can ready-cut, peeled tomatoes including juices
  (28 ounces)
4 or 5 jalapeño chiles, leaving some seeds
1 tablespoon minced garlic
1/2 cup diced red onion
1/4 cup cilantro
1/4 teaspoon salt
2 teaspoons vinegar

1. When tomatoes in the store are pink and hard, make this salsa. The canned tomatoes (S & W makes the ready-cut type) are the closest you can get to good fresh ones. Put the tomatoes and their juices in the bowl of a food processor. Add the garlic, jalapeños cut into pieces, and onion. Chop to a coarse puree.

2. Add the vinegar and salt. Simmer the salsa in an open saucepan for 10 minutes to concentrate the flavors. After you remove the salsa from the heat, stir in the cilantro. Makes 1 quart or about 8 servings.

Calories	27	Protein	1 gm
Fat	.3 gm	Carbohydrate	6 gm
Sodium	230mg	Cholesterol	0

MEXICAN CEVICHE SALAD

Because so many people are hesitant to eat raw fish, I prepare my recipe for Mexican ceviche using poached, chopped scallops and a lot of vegetables so it now resembles the conch salads served in the Carribean. Heaped in a huge shell, it makes a wonderful appetizer when paired with crackers or thin slices from a baguette.

1 pound large scallops
1 bottle clam juice
Juice from 1 lemon
1/2 cup red bell pepper, diced
2 tomatoes, diced
1/2 cup red onion, diced
1 jalapeño chile, seeds removed, diced
Juice of 3 limes
Juice of 1 orange
1 to 2 tablespoons olive oil
1/2 teaspoon dried oregano
2 tablespoons cilantro, snipped with scissors
Freshly ground pepper to taste

1. Bring clam juice and lemon juice to a simmer and add the scallops. Bring back to a gentle simmer and poach the scallops for 2 minutes. The idea is to just barely cook them. Do not walk away from the stove. Drain the scallops and cool. Chop Finely.

2. Meanwhile chop the tomato, onion, red pepper, and chile.

3. To the still warm scallops, add the lime and orange juice, the olive oil, oregano, and pepper. Stir in the chopped vegetables. Let the salad marinate for at least 2 to 3 hours before serving.

Serves 6 as an appetizer.

Calories	128	Protein	13 gm
Fat	5 gm	Carbohydrate	7 gm
Sodium	147 mg	Cholesterol	25 mg

RED SNAPPER FILETS VERACRUZ STYLE

During the five years we lived in central Mexico it was near impossible to obtain seafood, thereby only increasing our cravings for it. Our Mexican compadre, Eduardo, convinced us one Christmas vacation to spend a couple of weeks overdosing on seafood in the coastal town of Veracruz. We sat under the portales of the square and ate whole huachinango (red snapper) fried in butter for breakfast with cafe con leche and toasted bolillos; shrimp and oysters for lunch; for dinner, our most requested dish was huachinango veracruzano. After two weeks of this regimen, we were cured for awhile and ready to resume our highland diet.

Most often, in Mexico the red snapper is cooked whole in all of its glory but the filets cooked in sauce are also quite good and a lot speedier.

6 red snapper or rock cod filets, about 4 ounces each
2 teaspoons olive oil
1 can plum tomatoes and their juices (28 ounces)
1 cup chopped onion
1 teaspoon minced garlic
2 teaspoons red ground chile
1/8 teaspoon cinnamon
1/2 teaspoon sugar
2 teaspoons lemon juice
1 tablespoon orange juice
1/4 cup pimiento stuffed olives
1/4 cup pickled jalapeño chiles, sliced
Lemon or lime slices for garnish
Chopped parsley or cilantro for garnish

1. Chop the tomatoes in small pieces. Heat the olive oil and saute the onion and garlic until softened and then add the tomatoes. Stir in the rest of the ingredients and simmer all for about 15 minutes.

2. Preheat oven to 350 degrees. Place fish in a long baking dish with 1 cup of the sauce on the bottom. Spread the rest of the sauce over the top of the fish. Bake for 20 minutes and then check to see if fish barely flakes. If they are thick filets, they may need as much as 5 minutes longer.

3. Serve the fish in the baking dish garnished with the sauce, lemon or lime slices, and chopped cilantro or parsley. Huachingango Veracruzano is good with a simple rice dish or steamed new potatoes.
Serves 6.

Calories	176	Protein	25 gm
Fat	4 gm	Carbohydrate	9 gm
Sodium	516 mg	Cholesterol	42 mg

MICHAEL GRANT'S BOUILLABAISE CHILI

Whenever I serve this chili I have immediate requests for the recipe. If anyone was going to be sacrilegious about a chili dish, it might as well be a Texan as Texan as Michael, famous for his his cooking style, his column for the San Diego Union, and his claim that milk gravy has contributed substantially to his body type.

16 medium shrimp
1 can tomato sauce, 8 ounces
1 can tomato juice, 12 ounces
1 bottle clam juice, 8 ounces
3 red bell peppers
3 fresh Anaheim chiles
2 fresh jalapeño chiles
2 and 1/2 tablespoons cumin seeds
3 bay leaves
1 cup celery, chopped
1 cup onion, chopped

6 cloves garlic, minced through a press
1 tablespoon good chile powder (like Dixon)
2 teaspoons black pepper
Salt to taste
2 tablespoons olive oil
1 pound fresh red snapper fillets
1 pound fresh halibut
1/2 pound bay scallops
12 fresh mussels, bearded and scrubbed
1 to 2 cups water
1 bunch cilantro

1. Peel and vein the shrimp. Combine tomato sauce, tomato juice, clam juice and shrimp shells in a saucepan and simmer 15 minutes.

2. Under a broiler, roast the peppers and chiles until the skins are black all over. Steam the peppers and chiles in a paper bag for 5 minutes, then peel and seed them, and in a blender on low speed, reduce them to pulp.

3. Strain the shells from the tomato juice mixture, add the pureed peppers and chiles to the tomato juice, and continue to simmer. Toast the cumin seeds in a hot, dry skillet until golden and fragrant. Crush the seeds and bay leaves in an electric coffee grinder. I have one reserved just for spices.

4. Cut the fish fillets into 2-inch pieces. In a 6-quart pot, fry the vegetables and garlic in olive oil. Add the spices and fry 1 minute, stirring constantly. Add the fish and

shellfish and tomato-pepper mixture, and enough water to cover. Keep the stew on a low steady boil for 15 minutes. Add chopped cilantro during the last 5 minutes. Serve in large bowls with crusty French bread or fresh Mexican Bolillos. Sometimes when you prepare this it is difficult to find one of the fish or in particular, the fresh mussels. In this case, double up on the scallops or substitute something like squid. The last time I made the bouillabaise I found beautiful, cleaned Monterey squid. I just sliced the squid into rings and added it during the last 6 minutes of cooking and it was quite tender.
8 servings

Calories	355	Protein	37 gm
Fat	17 gm	Carbohydrate	13 gm
Sodium	615 mg	Cholesterol	87 mg

Note from Michael: if you double the recipe, do not double the jalapeños. *Michael Grant's Cookbook, Hearty Fare from a Country Kitchen* may be obtained from Cobble and Mickle. See Resources.

THE HOLY TRINITY

CHAPTER IV

 hat has been practiced in the Southwest since antiquity, is now recognized as healthful; the culinary trinity of **beans, corn, and chiles** are as necessary to the true native diet as air and water to survival. One element rarely exists without the other. An assortment of greens and vegetables are often merely seasoned with meats while large servings of meats and fowl are reserved for feast days and Sundays. Unfortunately,as with Mexican cooking, many Southwestern family recipes are laden with pork and lard and I have been told recently of many a family who has been warned to cut out the fat to save Papa's health. Even all the healthy beans and chiles cannot prevail against a high intake of fat. The fat, especially lard, adds a unique flavor and an unctuousness to the food. The tamales, made up of half their weight in lard, are creamier; the pozole with the pork shoulder and pigs' feet is richer in flavor; the tacos and Indian fry bread cooked in bubbly lard are crisper. Perhaps, for an occasional feast day or birthday dinner, the old food will always be there but for everyday, we all need to seriously cut back on the amount of hidden fat that works its way into our diets and seriously affects longterm health.

I am allowing the cooking trinity to guide my way through this chapter, beginning with beans.

Beans, the First of the Trinity

Beans have had a history of being subsistence food. My Spanish grandmother fed five hungry children beans and tortillas and bean sandwiches. After being overexposed to nouvelle foods, people are not only hungry for down-home foods, but beans are enjoying a gastronomic renaissance that tops all comfort food. Bean varieties, many of ancient stock which have previously hard-to-find, are now being offered. I am even tantalized by the old names - anasazi, ojo de cabra, flor de mayo, tepary, and azufrado.

If you send away for freshly harvested beans, from ranches or the Native Seeds Search in Tucson, you will be amazed at how quickly fresh, dried beans cook and how marvelous they taste.

The facts about beans make a good case for their health value: they average about 120 calories per half a cup and that amount will give you enough fiber to equal a bowl of oatmeal or a medium oat bran muffin.
Many oat bran muffins defeat their intent by being laden with fat and sugar, so that the advantages of the bran are relinquished.

Often, chili can be a bearer of fat-laden meats so I was challenged to come up with a version that would be so good and spicy, no one would miss the meat. First, I added the rich-tasting anasazi beans, my favorite, which can be obtained by mail order or in many health food stores. When beans are combined with pasta, rice, or other complex carbohydrates, they form a complete protein. Through the ages, it is obvious that combinations such as the red beans and rice of Louisiana and tortillas and beans of Hispanic cultures were instinctively wise.

IMPORTANT NOTE ABOUT DRIED BEANS

All dried beans contain greater and lesser amounts of complex sugars which can cause digestive problems in some people. The Bean Advisory Board encourages the hot soaking method which I have used throughout this book and which I use now to great success. By bringing the beans to a boil and simmering for at least 3 minutes and then soaking them for at least a couple of hours, you not only precook the beans but also throw away the soaking water which contains a large percentage of the irritating sugars. The discarded soaking water contains a minimum of the nutrients. I had read that another important maxim to follow with bean cookery is to thoroughly cook the beans. When I began work on this book, I purchased a very good stainless steel pressure cooker which I use for beans with overwhelming success. I really believe that this cooker makes the beans taste better, more velvety and richer and more digestible. I would not have believed it, had I not experimented with it on a daily basis. During the testing of this book, I averaged cooking a different type of bean recipe everyday for a couple of weeks. My freezer could feed a hoard of Mongolians. Even better, the pressure cooker finishes beans in 45 minutes and also produces rich chicken broth in about the same time. Do I sound like a convert?

The chili recipe below is so outstanding I urge you to banish any preconceived notions about vegetarian cooking. Carnivores are mad about this chile. The real secret to great chile is to use the best ground chile powders with superb flavor (such as Dixon and Chimayo), fresh spices, and herbs which you toast to bring out the flavors even more. Because of the combination of the beans, the bulgur, and the tofu, this chili packs a high amount of nutrients and would be a perfect food for discriminating marathoners.

DYNAMITE VEGETARIAN CHILI

1 pound anasazi or pinto beans
1 onion, chopped
2 cloves garlic, minced
● ● ● ● ● ● ● ● ● ● ● ● ● ● ● ● ●
2 teaspoons olive oil
3 cups chopped onion (about 2 onions)
1 tablespoon minced garlic
2 cups chopped red bell pepper (1 large pepper)
1 cup chopped green bell pepper (1 small pepper)
4 jalapeño chiles, seeded, minced
2 cans Italian plum tomatoes (28 ounces each)
1/4 cup ground chile like New Mexican Dixon
1 tablespoon toasted, ground cumin seed
1 tablespoon toasted, ground oregano
10.5 ounces of tofu (Mori-Nu), frozen and thawed
1/2 cup bulgur (cracked wheat)
2 cups corn niblets, canned or frozen

1. Cover the beans with water, bring to a boil and simmer for 3 minutes. Turn off the heat and allow to steep for 1 to 2 hours. Discard this soaking water. Because the beans turn out so creamy, I prefer covering them with 6 cups of fresh water, the chopped onion and garlic and pressure-cooking them for 45 minutes. If you do not have a pressure cooker, simmering the beans in a pot will take approximately 2 hours.

2. While the beans are cooking, prepare the rest of the chile. Toast the cumin seed in a heavy skillet just until there is a slight change of color, about 2 minutes. Add the oregano to the same skillet and toast for about a minute. Set aside. Chop the garlic, onion, red pepper, bell pepper, and jalapeño chiles. Coarsely puree the canned plum tomatoes in a blender or food processor.

3. Heat the olive oil in a large skillet and add the garlic and onion, sauteeing just until softened. Next add the peppers and chiles. Saute for 5 more minutes. Set aside

4. When the beans are cooked, stir in pureed tomatoes, the sauteed vegetables, the spices, and the chile powder. Simmer for 45 minutes to an hour.

5. Squeeze out the excess liquid from the thawed tofu. By freezing the tofu and then thawing it out, it crumbles more easily and blends well into sauces. Crumble the tofu and stir into the pot of simmering chile. At first, it will resemble grated Parmesan cheese and then it will start to take on the red of the chile. Add the bulgur at the same time. Simmer for 35 more minutes. Taste to adjust for seasonings. Add the corn during the last 15 minutes of simmering.
Serves 6.

Calories	553	Protein	32 gm
Fat	9 gm	Carbohydrate	95 gm
Sodium	504 mg	Cholesterol	0

BLACK BEAN CHILI AU GRATIN

If I was forced to choose my favorite between the Dynamite Vegetarian Chile or the Black Bean Chile, I could not. As often happens I choose my favorite that day by what I have in the cupboard or refrigerator. I have found that suppressed carnivores particularly love this chile because the golden crust of cheese satisfies their need for succulence. The three different types of chiles used add a marvelous dimension to the black beans which I often find less rich than anasazi or pintos and the pickled jalapeños, required here, add more clout than fresh jalapeños.

1 pound black beans, rinsed in a sieve
6 cups water
1 onion, chopped
1 bay leaf
• • • • • • • • • • • • • • • • •
2 teaspoons olive oil
1 and 1/2 cups chopped red onion
1 tablespoon minced garlic
1 tablespoon cumin seed, toasted
2 teaspoons oregano, toasted
1/2 cup canned, pickled jalapeño chiles, chopped
1 canned chipotle en adobo, minced
1 6-ounce can tomato paste
2 cups water
1/2 cup chile puree (made from 6 dried ancho, New Mexican, or California chiles (see below) or use canned chile puree
1/4 pound grated low-fat Jack or Mozzarella cheese

1. After rinsing beans, place in a large pot and cover with water. Bring to a boil and simmer for 3 minutes. Turn off heat and allow to soak for at least 2 hours. Pour off the soaking water. Place the beans in a pressure cooker and cover with 6 cups of fresh water, onion, and bay leaf. Pressure cook for 45 minutes. If you do not have a cooker, simmer the beans in a pot for about 1 and 1/2 hours or until tender.

2. While the beans are cooking, saute the chopped onions in the olive oil for 5 minutes. In a separate small pan, toast the cumin seeds over medium heat and then add the oregano. Remove the pan from the heat. The residual heat of the pan will bring out the flavor of the oregano. Add the spices to the onion. Also add the pickled jalapeño chiles and the chipotle chile. Saute all these ingredients together for about 5 more minutes and then stir into the beans when they are finished cooking.

3. Also add to the pot of beans, the tomato paste and extra water. Stir in the chile puree. For homemade chile puree simply wash off about 6 dried, red chiles. Break apart, remove stems, and shake out most of the seeds. Place in a heat-proof bowl and cover with boiling water. Place a lid over the bowl and allow to steep for at least 30 minutes. Place the soaked chiles in a blender or a food processor. Add 1/2 cup of the soaking water (if it is not bitter) or fresh water. Puree and push the chile puree through a wire strainer to remove bits of skin and seeds.

4. Simmer the Black Bean Chili for 45 minutes longer without a lid so the broth thickens and the flavors meld.

5. To serve, place in heat-proof bowls and sprinkle with about 1/4 cup of grated cheese. Place all of the bowls on a jelly roll pan and slide under a preheated broiler. Broil until the cheese is bubbly and has developed a golden crust.
Serves 6.

Calories	389	Protein	24 gm
Fat	7 gm	Carbohydrate	60 gm
Sodium	554 mg	Cholesterol	13 mg

A SIMPLE POT OF BEANS

Sometimes a rich and robust chili is not what you want. You want simplicity itself. Perhaps you want beans to go with barbecued meats or just with a thick slab of cornbread, one of my favorite combinations. If I am not adding a lot of other things to beans and I am not entertaining a vegetarian, I add a ham bone or something equally as good.

1 pound of beans - could be pinto, anasazi, kidney beans, red beans, small white beans, ojo de cabra
   (or a combination of many beans)
2 teaspoons olive oil
1 onion, chopped
1 teaspoon garlic, minced
1 ham bone, 8 ounces lean ham or Cajun tasso
1 teaspoon freshly ground pepper

1. Rinse beans in sieve and check for stones. Place in pot and cover with water. Bring to a boil and simmer for 3 minutes. Turn off the heat and allow the beans to steep for at least 2 hours. Pour off this soaking water and discard.

2. While beans are soaking saute the onion until just starting to brown. This will take about 10 minutes and then add the garlic. Stir the sauteed onions and garlic into the presoaked beans along with the rest of the ingredients. Lock on the lid of the pressure cooker, bring to correct pressure and simmer for 40 minutes.
Serves 8

Calories	244	Protein	17 gm
Fat	3 gm	Carbohydrate	37 gm
Sodium	411 gm	Cholesterol	106 mg

Note: tasso is a peppery (because of cayenne pepper), spicy Cajun smoked ham. The San Francisco sausage maker, Bruce Aidell, makes a lean version of this ham. Just small pieces of it can season the beans without adding excessive fat. See Resources for address.

BLACK BEAN PANCAKES

There are still surprises left in life and these can stand up and be counted. Bean pancakes were not invented by nouvelle chefs but by my grandmother who always had leftover beans. She would heat up her cast-iron pan with about a 1/2-inch of olive oil and drop in a cup of beans, mashing them and sizzling them at the same time. The bean pancake became crisp and golden around the edge and was wonderfully creamy in the center. My bean pancakes are an embellishment of hers minus a lot of olive oil. They are quite delicious with just a salad or quesadillas or even barbecued meats.

2 cups of cooked, drained black beans (can use canned)
1 clove garlic, minced
2 teaspoon olive oil
1 bunch green onion, minced
1 canned, pickled jalapeño chile, minced
1 teaspoon chile powder
1/2 teaspoon cumin seed, toasted and crushed
3/4 cup steamed barley (see step 2)
2 tablespoon cilantro, snipped
2 tablespoons olive oil
1 cup of cornmeal or oat bran for coating
1/2 cup low-fat sour cream
Salsa for a topping

1. Puree only 1/2 cup of the beans and stir in the remaining whole beans. Mash everything together. Saute the green onions in the 2 teaspoons of olive oil for 5 minutes. Add to the beans along with the jalapeño chile and the spices.

2. You can make the pancakes without the barley if your bean mixture is fairly stiff. The day I was testing this

101

recipe there was leftover steamed barley in the refrigerator. I liked its nuttiness and texture so I have added it here. To steam barley, bring 2 and 1/2 cups of chicken broth or water to a simmer and add one cup of dried barley. Add 1/2 teaspoon of salt. Steam for about 30 minutes on low heat or until all of the liquid is absorbed.

3. Stir the cooked barley and the cilantro into the black bean mixture.

4. Place the cornmeal or oat bran on a piece of wax paper. Spoon 1/4 cup of the bean mixture onto the coating of your choice and use a spoon to turn it over, flattening it into a patty. Heat the oil, preferably in a nonstick skillet, and add 3 pancakes. Saute about 2 minutes on each side and until golden brown. If you need more oil in the skillet, add only 1 teaspoon at a time. Serve each pancake with a teaspoon of low fat sour cream and some salsa.

Makes about 12 to 14 pancakes as an accompaniment to a dinner or lunch.

Calories	130	Protein	4 gm
Fat	4 gm	Carbohydrate	19 gm
Sodium	54 mg	Cholesterol	2 mg

NAVAHO BEAN SALAD

This bean salad was inspired by a superb, small book called *Pueblo and Navaho Cookery* by Marcia Keegan. I have lightened the dressing and added the cactus. Perfect for a summer barbecue, this salad is a welcome change from the generic, overly sweet bean salads. I often use one of the unusual native beans such as the brown tepary bean or the anasazi which cooks in half the time as the pinto. If you are pressed for time, you could use canned pinto or black beans, well-rinsed of their salty brine.

2 cups cooked pinto beans
2 cups cooked baby lima beans (frozen)
1 cup cooked green beans
2 cups cooked cactus (nopales) strips from jar, diced
1 and 1/2 cups sliced onion or bunch of green onions
2 teaspoons minced garlic
1 and 1/2 cups diced red bell pepper
1 teaspoon Dijon mustard
1 teaspoon sugar
1/4 teaspoon salt
1 teaspoon chile powder
1/4 cup oil
1/3 cup vinegar
1 teaspoon mild ground red chile (for sprinkling on top)

1. Mix all the vegetables together in a large bowl and then mix the dressing of mustard, sugar, salt, chile, oil, and vinegar. Toss the vegetables with the dressing and marinate for at least 2 hours. Before serving sprinkle the red chile on top for color.
Serves 8 as a side dish.

Calories	211	Protein	8 gm
Fat	8 gm	Carbohydrate	30 gm
Sodium	117 mg	Cholesterol	0

LENTIL CHILI

Lentils can quickly go from tiny ovals of texture to mush so the solution is to cook the sauce and lentils separately since the sauce needs more lengthy simmering.

2 teaspoons oil
1 and 1/2 cups chopped onion
1 cup chopped celery (2 stalks)
1 cup chopped carrots (2)
1 cup chopped green pepper
1 tablespoon minced garlic
3/4 cup minced green onions
1/2 pound ground turkey (7% fat) optional but great
1 and 1/2 cups peeled, chopped tomatoes
1 can tomato paste, 6 ounces
3 cups water
1/2 teaspoon ground cumin
1 teaspoon oregano
3 tablespoons ground red chile
1 cup peeled, diced jicama (added last 5 minutes)
1 cup dry lentils
3 cups water
1/2 teaspoon salt

1. Saute the chopped onion, celery, carrots, green pepper, garlic, and green onions until softened and then add the ground turkey and saute until the meat loses it pink color. Add all the rest of the ingredients except the jicama, lentils, and water. Simmer for 45 minutes

2. Rinse the lentils and simmer in 3 cups of water for 25 minutes. Drain off the cooking water and add lentils to the tomato mixture. Simmer the lentils in the tomato broth for 15 minutes and then stir in the diced jicama. Simmer for 5 more minutes and remove from heat so that the jicama remains crisp.

Serves 6 nicely with a salad.

Calories	210	Protein	12 gm
Fat	3 gm	Carbohydrate	37 gm
Sodium	478 mg	Cholesterol	0

CORN, THE SECOND FOOD OF THE TRINITY

Unlike California, where the native Indian and Spanish foods have disappeared from most tables, the real Southwest has prevailed particularly in New Mexico. If soup is the soul of Mexican cuisine, I would have to place corn dishes at the heart of the Southwest, especially posole. Ingredients used for centuries such as the white corn treated with lime and the blue corn of the Pueblo Indians have survived and are thriving. The Pueblo Indians, for centuries cultivated the blue corn still prominent in New Mexican cookery. This magical blueish- gray corn not only provides more nourishment than the yellow but also has an earthier, richer flavor.

The special lime-treated corn, known as nixtamal, hominy or posole, is especially rich in calcium and is the ingredient ground into masa used for corn tortillas, tamales, and the pupusas of Central America. The whole kernels are used to make posole stew. Posole is so important to feast days in both New Mexico and Mexico (spelled pozole there), it is often the focal point and most important food offered. With this book, I have carried on many inner battles between my tastebuds and my desire to discover a more healthful style of eating that I worried about the endangered species—the rich, fatty native dishes. Happily, through waging the battle stubbornly, I did not cast away posole, which unlike tamales, can considerably be reduced in fats.

In the past I was always served posole at a fiesta or a saint's day and there was a mystique about it, daunting me to ever try making it without the help of an entire village. I put off testing this recipe which is a blend of 10 different recipes minus the traditional pig's head, pigs' feet, and pork shoulder. The recipe below is far easier than most and it is my little triumph. It is so very good, it is one of the dishes I speak of when I say I could happily drown in the well of Mexican soups (and New Mexican stews).

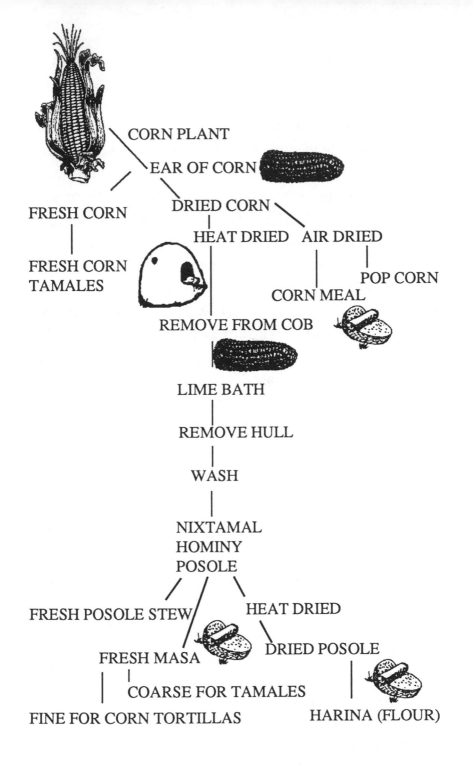

CORN PLANT

EAR OF CORN

FRESH CORN

DRIED CORN

FRESH CORN
TAMALES

HEAT DRIED   AIR DRIED

POP CORN

CORN MEAL

REMOVE FROM COB

LIME BATH

REMOVE HULL

WASH

NIXTAMAL
HOMINY
POSOLE

FRESH POSOLE STEW   HEAT DRIED

FRESH MASA   DRIED POSOLE

COARSE FOR TAMALES

FINE FOR CORN TORTILLAS   HARINA (FLOUR)

POSOLE

Note: remove all skin and large pieces of fat from chicken; use lean pork loin; refrigerate posole so you may lift off any fat in broth. Use fresh nixtamal (hominy) as it has a much more earthy and tasty flavor than canned hominy. Find a Mexican grocery store that sells masa and they will have fresh nixtamal. Nixtamal, hominy and posole kernels are all the same thing—the skinned whole kernels of corn which have been processed in a water bath treated with unslaked lime and calcium carbonate. The dried posole is an excellent substitute for the fresh and can be ordered by mail (see Resources) and purchased in some Mexican stores.

*1 pound of fresh or frozen nixtamal (hominy) or
    12 ounces of dried posole*
3 quarts of cold water
• •
2 and 1/2 pounds boneless, trimmed pork loin
2 cloves garlic, minced through a press
1 tablespoon ground red chile (Dixon is best)
*4 chicken legs with thighs attached, 2 and 1/2 pounds,
    skinned*
*2 cans reduced-sodium chicken broth (14 and 1/2 ounces
    each)*
1 quart water
1 large onion, chopped
1 head of garlic, rinsed well and top sliced off
2 bay leaves

2 teaspoons oregano

1 teaspoon cracked black pepper

1/2 teaspoon salt

2 dried red New Mexican chile pods, stemmed and seeded

2 teaspoons olive oil

1 cup chopped onion

1 teaspoon minced garlic

● ●

Condiments to Serve with Posole

2 cups of thinly sliced iceberg lettuce

1 bunch red radishes, thinly sliced

1/4 cup red ground chile

1 bunch green onions, sliced using half of the green tops

1/2 cup snipped cilantro

2 limes cut into small wedges

1. The day or night before you want to serve the posole, thoroughly cook the nixtamal by simmering. First place the kernels in a large sieve and rinse under cold, running water for several minutes. Discard any discolored kernels. Place in a 5-quart pot and cover with 3 quarts of cold water. If you are using dried posole, simply rinse in a sieve. Cover with cold water and cook for approximately 2 hours or until tender. Do not add anything else, particularly salt, which will prevent the kernels from softening during the cooking. Cook the nixtamal on low heat for 2 to 3 hours until softened and the kernels burst or "flower". They will still have a certain firmness to the bite. Remove from heat when cooked. Place in a large

bowl with some of the cooking liquid, cool down, and store covered in the refrigerator overnight.

2. The next day is posole day. Make sure you have removed all skin and fat from the chicken legs and thighs. You can leave them attached. My Mexican butcher thoughtfully leaves part of the backbone attached to the thigh. He believes this part adds great flavor. Place the chicken in a large pot containing the chicken broth, water, onion, head of garlic, bay leaves, oregano, crushed peppercorns, salt, and chile pods. Delete the salt if you are on a low-sodium diet. Simmer for about 45 minutes. Remove chicken to cool on a plate. This broth is heavenly and will taste as though you have labored for hours.

3. Fix the pork loin. Preheat the oven to 400 degrees. Rub the pork with the garlic and ground chile. Roast for 45 minutes on a rack or broiler pan so that any fat may drip away. Usually a fattier cut is boiled in the broth. I think the roasting step adds flavor and removes most of the fat although pork loin is now a very lean cut. Remove the roasted meat to a cutting board so it may cool.

4. Remove the cooled chicken from the bones and cut into small pieces. Cut the pork into 1-inch pieces. Place the chicken and the meat into the simmering broth. Drain the nixtamal of the watery liquid and add the kernels to the broth. Heat the oil in a pan and saute the chopped onion and garlic for about 8 minutes until softened and golden. Add to the pot of posole. Simmer

the posole for at least 45 more minutes once you have added everything to the pot.

5. You may chill the posole overnight. Using the above methods, you will not have much fat to remove from the top layer of the broth. The posole will become better in flavor and even freezes well.

6. When you are ready to serve, prepare all the condiments. All that is needed are good corn tortillas and cold beer.

Serves 10 (or 8 hearty eaters) This recipe doubles and triples very well if you are serving a fiesta of posole eaters.

Calories	440	Protein	44 gm
Fat	13 gm	Carbohydrate	35 gm
Sodium	756 mg	Cholesterol	124 mg

THE TAMALE PIE

Tamale pie always rises, like an old friend in a storm, along with reminiscence of childhood in the fifties. My grandmother and mother made superb versions of this dish (recipes in my California Rancho Cooking) but I have revised and defatted this old standby and it is one of those homey dishes that still I crave once in awhile.

1/3 cup cornmeal
1 teaspoon butter

1/4 teaspoon salt
1 cup + 2 tablespoons lowfat milk
1 egg, separated
1 egg white
2 tablespoons grated Asiago or Parmesan cheese

• •

1 teaspoon olive oil
1 and 1/2 pounds ground turkey (7% fat)
1 cup chopped onion
1 cup chopped bell pepper, red preferably
2 teaspoon minced garlic
1/3 cup raisins
4 ounces tomato paste
1 cup water
2 teaspoons ground red chile (more if you need it hot)
1 can Mexicorn (11 ounces)
1/2 cup black olives, sliced

1. First prepare the filling: saute the crumbled ground turkey in the olive oil, adding the onion, garlic, and bell pepper after the turkey has lost its pink color, about 10 minutes. Plump the raisins in hot water or place them in a small heat-proof dish, sprinkle with 2 tablespoons water and zap in microwave on high power for 40 seconds.

2. To the meat mixture, add the raisins and juice, tomato paste, water, and ground chile. Simmer this for 30 minutes and then stir in the corn and olives. Pour into a 1 and 1/2 quart baking dish. Set aside while you prepare the topping. Oven should be preheating to 375 degrees.

3. Heat milk, butter, and salt to a simmer. Stir in the cornmeal, blending well. Cook for about 2 minutes or until thickened. Remove from heat and beat the 2 egg whites to soft peaks. Stir the egg yolk and Parmesan into the warm cornmeal. Fold the beaten whites into the cornmeal mush. Gently spread over the meat mixture in the baking dish.

4. Bake for 30 minutes or until the top is starting to color. This topping creates a golden corn layer akin to a corn pastry which you will love.

Serves 6 .

Calories	365	Protein	27 gm
Fat	15 gm	Carbohydrate	32 gm
Sodium	708 mg	Cholesterol	125 mg

RANCHO COLACHE

This squash stew, an old recipe from my grandmother, is one of the most flavorful ways to treat zucchini and goes well with tamale pie or enchiladas.

3 teaspoons olive oil
1 cup chopped onion
1 and 1/2 pounds zucchini, sliced thickly
4 green chiles (Anaheim), charred, peeled,
*   seeded, chopped*
1 teaspoon minced garlic
1 cup chopped red bell pepper
1 cup canned, crushed tomatoes

1/2 cup water
1/2 teaspoon salt
4 ears of corn (2 ounces each)
For topping, 1 ounce grated Asiago cheese

1. Heat oil and saute onion until slightly softened, about 5 minutes. Push the onion to one side and saute the zucchini slices until golden. Keep turning every couple of minutes. It is this browning step that adds flavor and was so important to my grandmother's way of doing it. I have tried steaming all the vegetables together instead of sauteeing and the flavor is simply not there. The bottom heat of the frying pan bring out greater flavor than steaming.

2. Next add the chile peppers, garlic, red pepper, tomatoes, water, and salt. Bury the ears of corn within all of the vegetables. Place a lid on top of the pan and simmer everything on low for about 15 minutes.

3. Sprinkle the Asiago cheese on top, simmer for a couple of minutes or just enough time for the cheese to melt.

6 servings.

Calories	95	Protein	5 gm
Fat	4 gm	Carbohydrate	12 gm
Sodium	331 mg	Cholesterol	3 mg

CORN-BROWN RICE-LENTIL SALAD

For the simple days of the week, especially when I am busy, I keep this salad in the refrigerator for lovely sustenance.

1 and 1/2 cups cooked brown lentils
2 cups cooked brown basmati rice
1 can of corn niblets, 11 ounces
1 bunch chopped green onions, 1 cup
1 and 1/2 cups minced parsley
1/2 cup Jalapeño Vinaigrette (see recipe below)
1 teaspoon ground red chile (Dixon)
Strips of red pepper or pimiento

1. If you do not have on hand the cooked lentils, simply rinse 1 cup of dry lentils and place in a large pot with 2 quarts of cold water. Bring to a simmer and cook the lentils for 25 minutes. Do not overcook. Drain and rinse in cool water.

2. For the brown rice, I prefer my Japanese rice cooker; if you do not have a cooker simply bring to a simmer 2 and 1/2 cups water, 1 teaspoon low-sodium soy sauce, and add 1 cup of brown rice. Cook on low heat for 45 minutes. Do not lift the lid. Allow the rice to steam for 10 minutes with lid on after you have turned off the heat. Spread the rice out on a plate to cool before making the salad.

3. With a large fork, stir together the cooled rice, the lentils, onions, parsley, and corn. Sprinkle in the Jalapeño Vinaigrette and stir. I find it best to add 1/4 cup of the dressing now and then add more just before serving. Chill for at least 2 hours and then sprinkle with a little minced parsley and the ground chile. Some strips of red pepper also add the color that this brown salad needs. Serves 6 generously.

Calories	193	Protein	8 gm
Fat	4 gm	Carbohydrate	34 gm
Sodium	77 mg	Cholesterol	0

JALAPEÑO VINAIGRETTE

3 *tablespoon white wine vinegar*
3 *tablespoons lemon juice*
1/4 cup water
3 *tablespoon oil*
1 teaspoon Dijon mustard
1/4 teaspoon ground cumin
1 teaspoon garlic, minced
1 tomato, skinned and seeded
1 pickled jalapeño chile
1/4 cup cilantro

1. In a food processor, place all of the above ingredients and blend. Tiny bits of chile and cilantro give the dressing character. This dressing is also good on taco salad and green salads.
Makes 1 and 1/4 cups
See analysis on page 17

CORN ENCHILADAS

Surprise for people who think enchiladas are made of only cheese, beef, or chicken.

CHILE SAUCE:

2 ounces dried red New Mexican or California chiles, about 12
1 tablespoon oil
1 tablespoon flour
1/2 teaspoon ground cumin
1/2 teaspoon oregano
1/2 teaspoon sugar
1/2 teaspoon salt
1 cup reduced sodium chicken broth

CORN FILLING:

2 teaspoon oil
1 cup chopped onion
3 green Anaheim chiles, charred, skinned, seeded
1 red bell pepper, charred, skinned, seeded
2 cups corn kernels, fresh or frozen niblets
2 tablespoons low-fat sour cream (40 % less fat)
4 ounces reduced fat Monterey Jack cheese
1 ounce of reduced fat Monterey Jack cheese for garnish
6 flour tortillas or 12 corn tortillas

1. Make the Chile Sauce. Break apart the chiles, remove stems, and seeds. Rinse in cold water. Place in heat-proof bowl and pour boiling water over them. Place lid

on top of bowl and steep chiles for 30 minutes. Place the soaked chiles and 1 cup water in a food processor or blender and puree. Use a rubber spatula to rub the puree through a strainer to remove chile skins.

2. Heat the tablespoon of oil and stir in the flour until golden, about 2 minutes. Slowly stir in the chile puree, blending out lumps with the spatula. Add the spices, seasonings, and chicken broth. Simmer the sauce for 20 minutes. Set aside while you prepare the filling.

3. Char the chiles and red pepper under a broiler or over a gas flame until they are blackened. Saute the onion in the oil until softened and then stir in the chiles, peppers, and corn. Reserve 1/4 cup corn kernels for garnish. Simmer over low heat for 10 minutes. Remove from heat and stir in the sour cream and grated cheese.

4. Heat the tortillas on a griddle to soften. If you want to further cut the calories, use corn instead of flour tortillas. Place 1 cup of chile sauce on a dinner plate and arrange corn filling near by. Dip the tortilla, both sides, in the chile sauce. Place 1/4 cup corn filling (for flour tortillas) toward one edge and roll up. Place enchilada in a wide rectangular, lightly oiled baking dish. Leave at least 1/2-inch between each enchilada so they do not stick to each other and become difficult to remove later.

5. When all the enchiladas are completed, sprinkle them with a little grated cheese and the reserved corn. Bake in a preheated 350 degree oven for 15 minutes.

Serves 6.

Calories	324	Protein	14 gm	
Fat	11 gm	Carbohydrate	45 gm	
Sodium	765 mg	Cholesterol	18 mg	

Note: a wonderful, very Mexican addition to these enchiladas is to cook a diced red-skinned potato and carrot in an inch of water just until tender. Sprinkle with 2 teaspoons white wine vinegar. Place a few of the vinegary cubes of carrot and potato over each enchilada just before serving.

GREEN CORN TAMALES

I have searched for years for the perfect green corn tamale that is not laden with fat. It is quite easy to make a delicious tamale of fresh corn, lots of butter and shortening and cream. I made at least a dozen recipes before devising this one with a minimum of margarine and low-fat sour cream. These tamales are wonderfully succulent and I urge you to be creative with the filling such as using leftover chili for a change.

2 pounds frozen corn niblets, thawed
  or kernels cut from 12 ears of corn= 6 cups kernels
1 and 1/2 tablespoons sugar
1/2 teaspoon salt
1/3 cup melted corn oil margarine
1/4 cup low-fat sour cream
3/4 cup cornmeal

1/2 teaspoon baking powder
20 dried corn husks
24 pieces of 8-inch string
Tamale pot or large pot with steamer basket

FILLING:

1 zucchini, ends removed, cut into sticks
1 potato, cooked and diced
4 ounces reduced-fat Jack or Cheddar cheese, cut into
    sticks
2 Anaheim green chiles, charred, skin and seeds
    removed and cut into thin strips or use 2 canned
    chiles

1. Put the corn husks to soak in a sink filled with hot water. Soak for at least 15 to 20 minutes.

2. Puree 3 cups of the corn kernels in a food processor until fairly smooth. Dump into a large bowl. Add the next 3 cups of corn to the food processor and puree also. Next add the melted margarine, sour cream, sugar, and salt. Blend together briefly and then add to the bowl. Stir in the cornmeal and the baking powder.

3. Place a long length of heavy paper towel on the counter and place the husks on one end to drain. Have ready the corn batter, the filling, the lengths of string, and the tamale pot.

4. Place an opened corn husk in front of you. Spread 1/3 cup of corn batter in a 4" x 4" square on the husk, closer to one edge of the husk and leaving the bottom and top of the husk bare so it may be tied. Place a stick of zucchini, a cube of potato, a strip of green chile and a stick of cheese. Sometimes I sprinkle these with ground red chile for more color. Roll up the tamale, starting from the edge with the batter. Roll up gently. Place the tamale, seam side down and tie up each end with a piece of string. Place 4 or 5 opened corn husks on top of the steamer basket in the pot. You should have already added 2 inches of water to the pot. Lay each completed tamale on top of the bed of husks. You do not have to stand these tamales on their ends. Finish rolling the rest of the tamales. You should have at least 12. If you make them bigger, you might end up with 9 or 10.

4. Place the pot on the fire, bring to a boil, and steam the tamales on low heat for 35 minutes. Remove the tamales from the pot immediately.

Serves only 6 people who can easily eat 2 each.

Calories	199	Protein	6 gm
Fat	8 gm	Carbohydrate	28 gm
Sodium	232 mg	Cholesterol	8 mg

PAN DE MAIZ

On my family's land grant rancho in California, they served a corn and chicken dish that belonged in the realm of comfort food. It is quite wonderful using frozen corn niblets.

3 cups (12 ounces) light and dark chicken meat
  (removed from 1 and 1/2 pound roasted chicken)
16 ounce package frozen corn niblets, thawed
1/4 cup melted margarine
2 teaspoons sugar
1/4 teaspoon salt
1 tablespoon cornmeal
1/2 teaspoon sugar

1. Cut the chicken into large 2-inch pieces. Sometimes when I am in a hurry I buy a rotisserie-roasted chicken from the supermarket. As soon as you get the warm chicken home, pull off the skin and remove chicken from the bones. If you follow this procedure, the fat will not have a chance to penetrate the meat.

2. Using a food processor, puree the corn until smooth. Add the margarine, sugar, and salt. Blend quickly.

3. Lightly oil 2 long pans (7 and 1/2" x 13 "). Spread a thin layer of the pureed corn on the bottom. Place a middle layer of chicken, using the total amount. Spread the rest of the pureed corn on top. Sprinkle the top with the cornmeal and sugar.

4. Bake in a preheated 350 degree oven for 40 minutes or until the corn is golden around the edges.

Serves 6. A fruit salad is a perfect accompaniment.

Calories	254	Protein	19 gm
Fat	12 gm	Carbohydrate	19 gm
Sodium	230 mg	Cholesterol	50 mg

CHICKEN CHILI

Living out in the country, I have to go 25 miles into town. On shopping days I treat myself to lunch at The Whole Wheatery, a little health food store-restaurant where they concoct different soups and superb wholegrain breads each day. One winter afternoon they cheered me up with their fabulous chicken chile which served as the inspiration for this recipe although they probably don't cook their vegetables in beer! It is with spicy concoctions such as Chicken Chile that I became firmly convinced of how well one can eat without fatty ingredients.

3 and 1/4 pound chicken, skin removed
1 quart water
1 can beer (12 ounces)
1 cup of chopped celery, including leaves
1 cup chopped onion
1 tablespoon minced garlic

1 cup cooked beans (I prefer pinto or anasazi but use any
*   kind you like)*
1 can ready-cut tomatoes, 28 ounces
1 can Rotel tomatoes (10 ounces)
1 tablespoon oregano
1/4 cup mild or hot ground red chile
1 and 1/2 teaspoon ground cumin
1 cup frozen corn niblets
3/4 cup sliced black olives
1 cup reserved chicken broth from cooking chicken

1. I pressure-cook my chicken in 1 quart of water for 30 minutes. You could simmer the chicken for 45 minutes in a regular 5-quart pot. In the pressure cooker, the chicken remains juicy and the resulting broth is much better.

2. While the chicken is cooking, add the beer to a 5-quart pot along with the onion, celery, oregano, cumin, and garlic. Simmer until almost all of the beer is reduced to half its original amount. This step takes the place of sauteeing in oil.

3. While the onion mixture is cooking in the beer, roughly puree the tomatoes and Rotel tomatoes, a mixture of green chiles, onions, and tomatoes. If Rotel tomatoes are unavailable, substitute stewed tomatoes in the same amount. Add the tomato puree to the onions and beer. Stir in the ground chile and the cooked beans. Simmer for 30 minutes partially covered.

4. Cool the chicken (you should have about 32 ounces of chicken) on a plate and then remove meat from the bones. Chop in small pieces. Stir the chicken into the above chile mixture. Simmer for another 30 minutes, adding the cup of reserved broth. Add the corn (during all the cooking I remove the corn niblets from the freezer so they may thaw) and the olives. Simmer for 15 minutes longer.
Serves 8.

Calories	234	Protein	24 gm
Fat	6 gm	Carbohydrate	22 gm
Sodium	523 mg	Cholesterol	62 mg

BLUE CORN BANANA MUFFINS

Through two cookbooks I have searched far and wide for the most perfect blue corn muffin and the favorite has finally emerged from my testing.   It had to be sweet enough to balance the earthiness of the blue corn, light enough to be healthy and yet appealing to those dear souls (like my teenage sons) who see blue and run the other way.   The small amount of banana, the magic ingredient, gives a lovely moistness and sweetness. You can freeze the rest of the banana for breakfast drinks or pancakes or just stand there and eat it while the muffins are baking.

1 cup of blue corn flour (not blue cornmeal)
1/2 cup whole wheat pastry flour
1/2 cup unbleached all-purpose flour

2 teaspoons baking powder
1/2 teaspoon baking soda
1 tablespoon sugar
1/4 cup melted corn oil margarine
2 tablespoons honey
2 tablespoons mashed banana
2 egg whites
1/2 cup nonfat yogurt
1/2 cup lowfat milk (2%)

1.   Preheat oven to 400 degrees and spray a 12-cup muffin tin with Baker's Joy. Over a large bowl, sift together the blue corn flour (often referred to as blue corn atole in the Southwest), the whole wheat, the all-purpose flour, baking powder, baking soda, and sugar.

2. Melt the margarine. Stir in the honey.

3. In a small bowl, beat together the nonfat yogurt and milk until well-blended and then whisk in the egg whites. Next whisk in the mashed bananas so there are not any large lumps.

4. Pour the yogurt mixture over the dry flour mixture in the bowl and over this pour the melted margarine-honey mixture.   Mix just until blended and there are no dry spots. Do not overmix.

5. Spoon the batter into the 12 muffin cups and bake for about 14 to 15 minutes. The muffins will be a little golden around the edges when they are done. If you are

serving these for a party, it is fun to tear off 2-inch strips of dry corn husk and soak in hot water for 10 minutes to soften. Fit the husk strips into each muffin cup. Spray with Baker's Joy and spoon the batter over the husk. This is an attractive Southwestern way to bake the muffins.

Makes 12 medium muffins.

Calories	135	Protein	3 gm
Fat	4 gm	Carbohydrate	21 gm
Sodium	172 mg	Cholesterol	1 mg

PART IV CHILES, THE APEX OF THE TRINITY

If corn is the foundation of Southwestern foods then chiles are the key to unlocking the door to authentic, native cooking. In New Mexico as in Mexico, many of the most popular dishes revolve around chiles. A chile is not just a chile but a specific type, carrying with it a whole gamut of traits which dictate its destination - from mole to salsa.

A few years ago salsamania encouraged the average gringo to become more interested in chiles. With general interest heightened, more cooks are aware that chiles can go beyond salsa. While the commercial growers in southern New Mexico try to keep pace with the escalating appetite for chiles by growing milder strains, independent farmers on small plots nurse their native plants, often from seeds kept in families for generations. Perhaps it is the dry climate and the particular mounds of dirt where they are grown which bequeaths to them a richer flavor but I cannot live without the Chimayos and Dixons. When I am down to 1 pound of Dixon chile powder, I call up for more.

When you cook with flavorful, full-bodied chiles as opposed to the red dust often sold as chile powder, you will find that you need less salt in your cooking especially when the chile is combined with an abundance of garlic and spices.

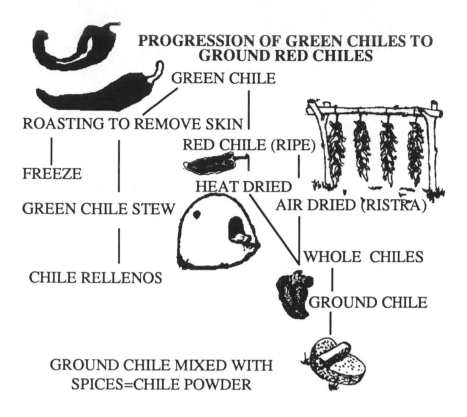

PROGRESSION OF GREEN CHILES TO GROUND RED CHILES

GREEN CHILE

ROASTING TO REMOVE SKIN

RED CHILE (RIPE)

FREEZE

HEAT DRIED

AIR DRIED (RISTRA)

GREEN CHILE STEW

WHOLE CHILES

CHILE RELLENOS

GROUND CHILE

GROUND CHILE MIXED WITH
SPICES=CHILE POWDER

GREEN CHILE STEW

Of all the unusual things I'm always concocting in my
kitchen, this stew is my sons' favorite. They love the
chunks of browned meat, carrots, and potatoes—all
identifiable foods where their mother doesn't appear to
have hidden anything suspicious. This is one of the most
widely eaten stews in the Southwest.

1 and 1/2 pounds pork tenderloin
2 teaspoons ground red chile
2 teaspoons ground cumin
1 tablespoon oregano
2 teaspoons oil
1 cup chopped onion

1 tablespoon minced garlic

3 cups homemade chicken stock or reduced sodium chicken broth

1 bay leaf

1/4 cup pickled jalapeño chiles, chopped

1/2 pound Anaheim green chiles (about 4), charred, peeled, chopped

1 pound red-skinned potatoes, cut in half

1 bunch carrots, about 2 cups cut into 3" pieces

1. Cut the meat into 3-inch chunks and rub with the chile, cumin, and oregano. Heat the oil in a heavy 5-quart pot (I use a Le Cruset enameled cast-iron pot) and brown the meat chunks 3 batches at a time, removing it as it is browned. When all the meat is ready, saute the onion until softened. Next stir in the garlic, the stock, and the bay leaf. Put all of the browned meat back into the pot. Simmer for 30 minutes.

2. While the meat is simmering, prepare the chiles by charring and removing the skins and seeds. Chop the chiles and stir into the meat along with the chopped jalapeños.

3. Prepare the vegetables and add them to the pot. Simmer until they are tender, 20 to 25 minutes. Serve meat and vegetables with some of the chile broth in wide soup bowls. Blue corn muffins or cornbread is a perfect accompaniment.

6 servings

Calories	271	Protein	27 gm
Fat	6 gm	Carbohydrate	27 gm
Sodium	172 mg	Cholesterol	74 mg

TURKEY BREAST GREEN CHILE STEW

Here is another version of the traditional green chile stew.

2 and 1/2 pounds turkey breast, skin and bone removed
2 teaspoons olive oil
1 cup chopped onion
2 teaspoons minced garlic
6 green Anaheim chiles, charred, skins and seeds re moved or 2 cans green chiles (7 ounces each)
2 teaspoons oregano
1 bay leaf
1/4 teaspoon cinnamon
3 teaspoons dried ground green chile (see Resources)
4 cups reduced sodium chicken broth or homemade chicken broth
2 sweet potatoes, 12 ounces
1 tablespoons flour
1/4 cup light sour cream (40% fat)
1/2 avocado, 8 slices for garnish

1. Cut turkey into large 2-inch chunks and dry well with a paper towel. Heat the oil and brown the turkey in 3 batches, removing pieces from pan as they brown. Next add the onion to the pan and saute until softened. Stir in the garlic. Chop the chiles and add to pan along with the spices and chicken broth. The dried green chile adds great flavor but the stew will still be good without it. Simmer the turkey for 20 minutes.

2. Add the sweet potato chunks and simmer for 20 minutes longer.

Stir the flour into the sour cream and blend this mixture into the simmering broth. Gently cook for 2 minutes and remove from heat.

8 servings.

Calories	219	Protein	29 gm
Fat	5 gm	Carbohydrate	14 gm
Sodium	115 mg	Cholesterol	70 mg

SANTA FE STROGANOFF

Beef eaters rejoice, I have not forgotten your existence. Flank steak, when marinated and cut on on the cross-grain, is quite tender and very flavorful. Best of all, it is a leaner cut.

1 flank steak, 1 and 1/2 pounds
2 teaspoons olive oil
1/4 cup red wine vinegar
1 teaspoon low sodium soy sauce (7.6 % sodium)
2 teaspoons Worcestershire sauce
1 teaspoon oregano
1 teaspoon black pepper
1 teaspoon minced garlic
4 green chiles, charred, skins and seeds removed, chopped
  or use canned chiles
1 can reduced-sodium chicken broth
1 pound button mushrooms
1/2 cup light sour cream (40% less fat)
1/4 cup cilantro, snipped with scissors
2 teaspoons ground red chile

1. Slice the flank steak across the grain into 1/2-inch slices and then cut the slices in half, into strips. Make a marinade of the olive oil, vinegar, soy sauce, Worcestershire sauce, oregano, black pepper, and garlic. Rub this into the meat strips and marinate for at least a couple of hours.

2. In a separate skillet, simmer the chopped green chiles and chicken broth for 15 minutes.

3. After the meat has marinated spray a saute pan with Pam and quickly sear the meat strips in 3 batches. Remove each batch to the skillet containing the chiles. Simmer all of the browned meat in the chile-broth for 15 minutes.

4. Wash the mushrooms quickly under running water. Wipe clean with a soft paper towel and slice. Meanwhile, add 1 teaspoon of olive oil to the saute pan you used for the meat. Saute the mushrooms for 2 minutes. Add to the meat during the last 5 minutes of simmering. Stir in the sour cream and half of the cilantro, reserving the rest for garnish. Do not simmer the sour cream too long or it will curdle. Place the Stroganoff in a serving dish and sprinkle with minced cilantro and a couple of teaspoons of ground red chile. This dish is quite good when served over noodles, especially red pepper or chile noodles.

6 servings

Calories	316	Protein	26 gm
Fat	19 gm	Carbohydrate	10 gm
Sodium	349 mg	Cholesterol	66 mg

HEALTHY TORTILLAS

I would be thrown out of the family if I admitted liking anything other than flour tortillas (I'm admitting to you that I can go through a stack of fresh, warm blue corn tortillas like I never heard of calories) I have tried to make my grandmother's rancho flour tortillas healthier and my tasters love this version the very best. You have to sneak in the whole wheat otherwise you end up with a doughy tortilla. Besides having a superior flavor and delicacy, homemade tortillas are not loaded with lard, bleached flour, and preservatives. Many store-bought flour tortillas contain a high amount of fat in order to keep them soft.

3 and 1/2 cups unbleached all-purpose flour
1/2 cup pastry whole wheat flour
1 teaspoon salt
1/2 teaspoon baking powder
1/4 cup soft corn oil margarine
1 and 1/2 cups warm water

1. Sift together both the flours, the salt, and baking powder.

2. Using a large fork or pastry blender, mix the margarine into the flour mixture as though you were mixing pastry. I often end the mixing using my finger tips to assure that the fat is well distributed.

3. Slowly add the water until you have a soft dough. Knead the dough for 1 minute right in the bowl, dusting the top of the dough with a little flour if it seems too sticky. Place plastic wrap over the bowl and let the dough rest for 30 minutes to a couple of hours.

4. After the rest, oil your hands and a jelly roll pan. Form the dough into 14 balls. Place the balls on the pan and flatten into 3-inch discs and allow them to rest at least 30 minutes, covered with plastic wrap so they do not dry out. This rest can be up to several hours or overnight in the refrigerator. It is an imperative step because it allows the gluten in the dough to relax and it will be easy to roll out each tortilla.

5. When you are ready to roll out tortillas, preheat a griddle preferably of cast-iron or rolled steel and 10 to 12 inches wide. Lightly dust your board with flour and place flattened tortilla ball in center, keeping the rest of the balls covered so they do not dry out. Begin rolling the dough into a thick circle. Make a quarter turn of the tortilla after each two short strokes and your tortilla will remain round. A standard rolling pin is not as easy to roll with as a 1-inch dowel, about 7 to 8 inches long. A sawed-off broom handle is perfect.

6. After you have rolled an 8-inch circle, you can now hand stretch your tortilla into a 10-inch circle. Hang the tortilla from the fingertips of one hand, drawing the fingertips of the other hand across the bottom of the tortilla, pulling and stretching toward you. Perform this

stretching 2 times in each direction across the tortilla to make it thin. You cannot achieve this by just rolling the dough on a board for the same reason that pizza makers never just roll out their dough but finish it off by tossing it in the air. Enchiladas made with these hand stretched tortillas will be as light as though you had used crepes. Store-bought tortillas cannot match the delicacy.

7. Cook the tortilla on the preheated, hot griddle with a medium flame under it. Keep turning the tortilla every 10 seconds for about a minute. As it cooks, it will puff in spots and begin to develop golden freckles. Do not push on the tortilla as it is puffing as it is forming layers just as pastry would. You usually have to turn the tortilla 4 or 5 times before it is done. Wrap the completed tortillas in a tea towel. When you have cooked them all, place the wrapped tortillas inside a plastic bag so they do not dry out. Placing warm tortillas inside plastic immediately causes them to sweat.

Makes 14 large 10-inch flour tortillas.

Calories	157	Protein	4 gm
Fat	4 gm	Carbohydrate	27 gm
Sodium	211 mg	Cholesterol	0

VEGETABLE BURRITOS WITH KILLER RED SAUCE

Vegetarian foods have an insipid reputation. For instance, a vegetable burrito should be covered with the same kind of sauce you would put over any delightfully greasy carnita (fried pork bits) burrito. If you are going to win over an occasional carnivore, you will not do it using kid gloves. The idea is to use a sauce that will have them breathless and they won't care what's inside the burrito. A few years back, when my twin sons turned eight they decided to hate vegetables unless they were encased in 1000 calories of cheese sauce. Now that they are seventeen, they are beginning to consider the possibility of vegetables being more than French fries. Recently, I served them Vegetable Burritos covered with Killer Red Sauce for lunch. Since they were reading, they were not watching as they shoveled in huge bites. O'Reilly spotted a green cube of zucchini. He said, "Mom, you've tricked us. This is illegal." But he kept eating.

2 teaspoons olive oil
1 cup red onion, chopped
1 and 1/2 cup mixed frozen vegetables
 1/4 cup roasted red bell peppers from jar
1 cup diced zucchini
1/2 cup Jacquie's Everyday Salsa or store-bought
8 ounces of grated mozzarella cheese
6 flour tortillas (10-inch)
Killer Red Sauce, recipe below

1. Heat the olive oil in a nonstick skillet and saute the onion on very low heat for 15 to 20 minutes or until soft and carmelized. This onion marmalade will add considerable flavor to any steamed vegetables.

2. Steam together the mixed frozen vegetables, the red peppers, and the diced zucchini for about 10 minutes until just tender. Use a saucepan with a steamer basket if possible. The last minute of steaming, sprinkle the mozzarella cheese over the top of the vegetables. Watch carefully as the cheese will melt in less than a minute and you do not want it to drip down into the steaming water! Place the steamed vegetables and cheese into a bowl and stir in the salsa and sauteed onions.

3. Warm each flour tortilla just enough on a griddle so you may fold it into the burrito without cracking. Place a scant 1/2 cup of vegetable-salsa filling down the middle of the tortilla. Fold over each end of burrito and then fold one side to the center over the filling and then the other side. Place on a plate and cover with warmed Killer Red Sauce or briefly heat the folded burrito on the hot griddle and serve it naked. Just douse it with more salsa.

Calories	279	Protein	13 gm
Fat	10 gm	Carbohydrate	34 gm
Sodium	384 mg	Cholesterol	29 mg

KILLER RED SAUCE

Dried red chiles can sometimes be too potent unless you were born in New Mexico or you are one of those converts more avid than the natives. By simmering the dried chiles with tomato, onion, and garlic the chiles are sweetened and I think their flavor is boosted. Without a doubt, this has become one of my favorite red sauces.

12 dried red chiles (New Mexican, California,
  ancho), about 3 ounces
4 cups water
1 /2 cup chopped onion
3 cloves whole, unskinned garlic
1 and 1/2 cups chopped, unskinned tomatoes
  (about 8 ounces)
1/4 teaspoon salt
1/2 teaspoon sugar

1. Place the dried chiles on a baking sheet and toast in a preheated 250 degree oven for 8 minutes. Do not toast them too much or the chiles will become bitter. Remove and place in a sink filled with cold water. Rinse the chiles off. Remove stems and seeds.

2. Simmer chiles, tomatoes, onion, and garlic, salt and sugar in water for 30 minutes. Cook with the lid on and every 5 minutes push the chiles back down into the liquid. The chiles will absorb a lot of the liquid.

3. Puree everything in a food processor (in 2 batches) and push through a wire strainer to remove skins.

4. Simmer the sauce in a skillet for at least 5 minutes to concentrate flavors.

Makes approximately 2 and 1/2 cups chile sauce or 1/4 cup servings for 10 enchiladas or burritos. Freezes beautifully.

Calories	36	Protein	1 gm
Fat	1 gm	Carbohydrate	7 gm
Sodium	59 mg	Cholesterol	0

CHICKEN COLORADO

Chile colorado is one of my husband's favorite Mexican dishes but it is usually made with a cut of meat that is very fatty. This is one of those instances when having a refrigerator of sauces from my numerous testings has come in handy. I combined chunks of poached chicken with the Killer Red Sauce above and came up with Chicken Colorado, which makes great burritos especially if you have some beans on hand.

3 cups light and dark chicken meat, removed from 1 and 1/2 pound poached chicken
2 and 1/2 cups Killer Red Sauce (see recipe above)
1 teaspoon toasted cumin seeds, ground

1. To poach a chicken, use the directions for Easy, Friendly Chicken Broth on page 42 but reduce 20 minutes from the cooking time, removing the chicken early even if you are using a pressure cooker.

2. Remove the cooked chicken from the bones and cut into large 2 or 3-inch chunks. Place in a 3-quart pot with the Killer Red Sauce and cumin. Simmer on low for 30 minutes with lid partially on. Stir frequently as chile sauce tends to stick and burn. If sauce becomes too thick, add 1/2 cup poaching liquid from chicken or plain water. 4 servings or 6 burritos using 10-inch flour tortillas

Calories	252	Protein	28gm
Fat	10 gm	Carbohydrate	17 gm
Sodium	220 mg	Cholesterol	76 mg

ENCHILADAS OF THE JARDIN

The first year I lived in San Miguel de Allende, Mexico I often strolled the jardin at dusk. The cooking women, in front of their smoky braziers, were like figures in the pattern of an old tapestry. I often lingered to watch each woman's cooking style, listening to their banter as they patted thick corn tortillas, rolled them around a scant bit of crumbled goat's cheese and bits of raw onion and then sizzled them blackened skillets. The enchiladas were hot in a minute and rolled out onto a terra cotta plate. If I remained too long, captivated by the skillets, the women knew I could not resist their offerings.

For this I paid dearly a few years later when I had to be attended to by a French doctor in Mexico City who worked miracles and spoke against the dangers of street food, unpeeled tomatoes, and swamp gardens.

Sometimes when we are barbecuing, I put a heavy cast-iron skillet at one end of the grill and cook these enchiladas. Somehow they must be imbued with mesquite smoke to taste exactly right.

2 and 1/2 cups Killer Red Sauce (see page   )
3/4 cup crumbled farmer's cheese (or goat's cheese)
1/2 cup chopped onion
3 carrots, diced
2 red-skinned potatoes, diced
1 bay leaf
1 tablespoon cider vinegar
Pink Pickled Onions (see recipe, page   )
12 corn tortillas

1. Soak the chopped onion in cool water while you prepare everything else. Simmer the carrots and potatoes in water to cover with the bay leaf for about 15 minutes or just until tender. Remove to a plate and sprinkle with the vinegar while still warm. Add the Pink Pickled Onions to the plate.

2. Warm 1 and 1/2 cups of the Killer Red Sauce in a heavy 12-inch skillet, preferably cast-iron. Drain the chopped onion and pat dry.

3. Spray a nonstick skillet with oil and heat one tortilla at a time. When the tortilla is warm and pliable, dip in the red sauce and place on a flat plate. Sprinkle 1 tablespoon cheese and a teaspoon of onion down the middle. Roll up into a tube or enchilada.

4. Add more red sauce to the skillet and heat 6 enchiladas at a time. This won't take long, maybe just a minute. Place 2 enchiladas on each plate and sprinkle with some of the diced carrots and potatoes and a couple of rings of Pink Pickled Onions.

12 enchiladas for 6 people.

Calories	150	Protein	6 gm
Fat	4 gm	Carbohydrate	26 gm
Sodium	155 mg	Cholesterol	5 mg

EGGPLANT ENCHILADAS

I am resurrecting these enchiladas from my California Rancho cookbook because they are so good. People have actually mistaken the pieces of eggplant for meat.

2 and 1/2 cups of Killer Red Sauce, see page 139
3 teaspoons olive oil
1 and 1/2 cups chopped onion
2 cups of peeled, diced eggplant
3 teaspoons oregano
1 cup grated reduced fat Cheddar cheese
12 corn tortillas
Pam for spraying saute pan
1/2 cup lowfat, plain yogurt
1/4 cup minced green onions

1. Heat the olive oil in a nonstick skillet and saute the onions until they are very soft, about 20 minutes.

2. Meanwhile, place the eggplant cubes in a vegetable steamer. Steam for 8 minutes. Blot off excess moisture with paper towels and add to the skillet containing the sauteed onions. Cook the onions and eggplant together for about 10 minutes, adding the oregano.

3. Spray a nonstick skillet with Pam and heat each corn tortilla just enough to soften. Dip both sides of the tortilla in Killer Red Sauce. Place 1/2 cup of sauce at a

time in a dinner plate to facilitate dipping. Add a couple of tablespoons of eggplant-onion mixture and a tablespoon of grated cheese.

4. Roll up the enchiladas and place in a long, greased baking dish which you have oiled. Bake in a preheated 350 degree oven for 15 minutes or until cheese is melted. Do not bake too long or you will end up with a casserole.

5. Stir the minced green onions into the yogurt and use for garnish over each enchilada.
Makes 12 enchiladas for 6 people

Calories	156	Protein	7 gm
Fat	5 gm	Carbohydrate	22 gm
Sodium	176 mg	Cholesterol	7 mg

GREEN CHICKEN ENCHILADAS

These enchiladas are done with my new great discovery, Tomatillo Salsa with tomatillos cooked in the microwave.

1 and 3/4 pound poached or roasted chicken,
    skin removed with 12 ounces of light and dark meat
3 cups Fast Tomatillo Salsa (recipe below)
2 teaspoons oil
1 cup chopped onion
1/2 cup diced green chiles, fresh or canned
1 cup grated reduced fat Monterey Jack cheese
1/2 cup light sour cream (40% less fat)

3 tablespoons low-fat milk (2% fat)
1 tablespoon minced green onion
2 teaspoons oil
12 corn tortillas

1. To poach a chicken, use the directions for Easy, Friendly Chicken Broth on page 42 but subtract 20 minutes from the cooking time of the broth and remove the chicken early even if you are using a pressure cooker. If you are in a great hurry, you can buy a rotisserie-roasted chicken from the supermarket. Don't chill it unless you remove the fatty skin first.

2. Remove the chicken from the bones. Heat the oil in a saute pan and cook the onions over low heat until softened. Add the green chiles and cook together for about 5 more minutes. Fresh green chiles that have been charred and peeled have the most flavor but use canned chiles if you are in a hurry. Set aside and stir in chicken.

3. Blend milk, sour cream, and green onion together and set aside.

4. Heat 1 teaspoon of oil in a nonstick 10-inch skillet. Warm each tortilla in the skillet until it is soft and pliable. Have ready your chicken-chile filling and a dinner plate holding about 1/2 cup Fast Tomatillo Salsa. Dip both sides of the tortilla in the salsa (which will only lightly coat it) and place about 2 tablespoons of the chicken-chile filling in each tortilla. Roll up and place in an oiled baking dish. You will need 2 baking dishes for 12

enchiladas or 1 jelly-roll pan. Sprinkle grated cheese over the tops of the enchiladas and bake in a preheated 350 degree oven for 15 minutes. During the last 5 minutes of baking, drizzle the sour cream over all. You have to be careful about overbaking enchiladas made out of tortillas that have not been heavily fried as they tend to fall apart more. Pour more heated salsa over the enchiladas just before serving.

Makes 12 enchiladas for 6 people.

Calories	201	Protein	15 gm
Fat	8 gm	Carbohydrate	18 gm
Sodium	174 mg	Cholesterol	35 mg

FAST TOMATILLO SALSA

This salsa works better with tomatillos prepared in a microwave than any other way I have tried. The tomatillos remain sweeter and brighter.

1 and 1/2 pounds tomatillos
1/2 cup chopped onion
4 jalapeño chiles, stems and some seeds removed
3 cloves garlic, in pieces
1/2 cup cilantro
1 teaspoon vinegar
1/4 teaspoon salt
1/2 teaspoon sugar

1. Soak tomatillos in a sink full of warm water to soften the dry husks. After 2 minutes of soaking, peel off the husks. Place tomatillos on a flat dinner plate and microwave on high power for 225 seconds (for a 600 watt oven).

2. Place the tomatillos in a food processor and chop roughly and add the rest of the ingredients and puree. I always leave some of the veins and seeds in the chiles because tomatillos have a mysterious way of obliterating hot chiles. If you like really hot green sauce, you may find yourself adding at least 1 more chile to those required in the recipe. Maybe you'll want to add 2 more chiles!
Makes 1 quart of salsa or 16 servings.

Calories	15	Protein	.7 gm
Fat	.2 gm	Carbohydrate	3 gm
Sodium	34 mg	Cholesterol	0

SPICY TURKEY TENDERLOINS WITH RED PEPPER SAUCE

Cooking turkey tenderloins with the beer method retains the juiciness of the meat rather than drying it out as roasting can sometimes do. Sometimes I serve these with both the Fast Tomatillo Salsa and the Red Pepper Sauce. Rice or noodles are a perfect accompaniment.

2 turkey tenderloins, 12 ounces each
1 teaspoon granulated garlic
1 teaspoon oregano
2 teaspoons ground chile
1/4 teaspoon salt
1 teaspoon dried thyme leaves
2 teaspoons oil
1 cup room temperature beer
2 red bell peppers
2 teaspoons olive oil
2 cloves garlic, minced through press
1/4 cup chopped onion
1 tablespoon tomato paste
1 teaspoon dried thyme leaves
1/2 cup dry white wine
1 cup low sodium chicken broth
1 tablespoon low-fat sour cream (40% less fat)
1/4 cup parsley, minced

1. Blend all the spices together and rub over the tenderloins. Let them marinate at room temperature while you prepare the Red Pepper Sauce.

2. Char the red peppers over a gas flame or under a broiler until they are completely blistered and blackened. Steam them for 10 minutes in a plastic bag and then scrape the skins off with a small knife and cut out the stems and cores. Cut the peppers into small pieces.

3. Saute the onion and garlic in the oil for 5 minutes and then add the red peppers and saute for a couple of minutes. Next add the tomato paste, the thyme, the wine, and the chicken stock. Simmer for 10 minutes, until reduced by half. Place everything in a food processor and puree. Remove and stir in the sour cream. Set aside while you cook the turkey tenderloins.

4. Heat the oil in a nonstick skillet that has a tight-fitting lid. Add both of the tenderloins and saute about a minute on each side or just enough to lightly brown. Add the cup of beer and clamp on the lid. Simmer the tenderloins for a total of 20 minutes. Every 5 minutes turn them and push around in the beer sauce. This is also a great way to cook strips of boned chicken breast for fast fajitas.

5. Serve slices of the turkey with warm **Red Pepper** Sauce, sprinkled with minced parsley.
6 servings

Calories 191	Protein	28 gm
Fat 6 gm	Carbohydrate	6 gm
Sodium 210 mg	Cholesterol	71 mg

CHICKEN RAPIDO

Everyone adores this simple recipe and best of all it's easy on the cook. All you need is a tossed salad.

1 cup finely ground unsalted tortilla chips
1 cup finely ground flaked wholewheat cereal
  (Nutri-grain)
1 package taco seasoning (1 and 1/4 ounces)
2 egg whites
24 ounces of boned, skinned chicken breasts,
  cut into strips
1 and 1/2 tablespoons melted margarine

1. Grind the tortilla chips and the cereal together in a food processor.
Place the crumbs in a flat dinner plate. Mix the taco seasoning into the crumbs.

2. Beat the egg whites with a fork until they are foamy.

3. Dip the chicken strips into the egg whites and then into the crumbs.

4. Place on a jelly roll pan sprayed with Pam. After all of the chicken strips are coated, drizzle with the margarine. Bake in a preheated 350 degree oven for about 18 minutes until chicken strips are golden and crispy.
6 servings.

Calories	270	Protein	30 gm
Fat	8 gm	Carbohydrate	18 gm
Sodium	536 mg	Cholesterol	66 mg

SOFT TACOS WITH SALSAS

Soft tacos are the only tacos I remember in Mexico and now in Southern California there are a burgeoning number of joints that grill marinated chicken and beef, fold them into warm corn tortillas, and allow you to find your way through a salsa bar. But now you can make them at home.

24 ounces of skinned, boned chicken breast
2 tablespoons lemon juice
2 teaspoons olive oil
1 teaspoon minced garlic
1/2 teaspoon salt
1/2 teaspoon black pepper
1/4 cup chopped onion
1/4 cup minced cilantro
12 corn tortillas

1. Marinate the chicken breast meat in lemon juice, olive oil, garlic, salt, and black pepper.

2. Broil or grill about 4 to 5 minutes per side. Place the grilled chicken on a chopping board and chop into small pieces. Mix up the chicken with the onion and cilantro.

3. Warm tortillas on a griddle or in a microwave just until soft and warm.

4. Place chicken filling in the middle of each tortilla and let each person add his choice of salsa: Fast Tomatillo

Recipes for Hacked-up Salsa and Jacquie's Everyday Salsa are given below.

Makes 12 soft tacos for 6 people although I've known some men who can eat 4.

Calories	138	Protein	15 gm	
Fat	2 gm	Carbohydrate	13 gm	
Sodium	182 mg	Cholesterol	33 mg	

HACKED-UP SALSA

3 medium tomatoes, diced
1/2 cup diced white onion
1 jalapeño chile, minced (include seeds in this salsa)
1 avocado, skinned, seed removed, diced
3 teaspoons lime juice
1/4 teaspoon salt
1 tablespoon cilantro

1. Mix everything together and serve immediately. If you like it hot add another chile.

3 cups salsa for 6 servings because everyone eats it like salad.

Calories	72	Protein	1 gm	
Fat	5 gm	Carbohydrate	7 gm	
Sodium	100 mg	Cholesterol	0	

JACQUIE'S EVERYDAY SALSA

There is always a big jar of this medium-hot salsa in my refrigerator because I stir it into anything that needs a lift.

4 ounces tomatillos
2 pounds tomatoes
1 cup chopped onions
1/2 cup chopped green onions
1 tablespoon minced garlic
1/2 cup green chiles from can (about 2 chiles)
1/2 cup jalapeño chiles, some seeds removed
2 teaspoons ground red chile
1/2 teaspoon ground cumin
1/2 teaspoon salt
1/2 cup minced cilantro
3 tablespoons white wine vinegar

1. Soak the tomatillos in warm water and remove the dry husks. Dip the tomatoes in boiling water for 30 seconds to loosen the skins or hold over a gas flame and char. Remove the skins and squeeze out seeds.

2. Roughly puree everything in food processor.

3. Simmer in an open 2-quart saucepan for 5 minutes to blend favors and help preserve the salsa. Salsa keeps well. If you want the salsa even hotter, just dice 2 more chiles, including the veins and seeds.

Makes 5 and 1/2 cups

Calories	16	Protein	.6 mg
Fat	.1 gm	Carbohydrate	3 gm
Sodium	75 mg	Cholesterol	0

INSIDE-OUT QUESADILLA WITH
SMOKED FIRE

Quesadillas are survival food. Instead of folding the tortilla over grated cheese, as is usually done, these quesadillas are painted with a smoldering salsa first. When you are in a hurry and think you are starving hungry, this is what you need. These also give you a salsa fix.

2 flour tortillas (8-inch)
4 tablespoons Smoked Fire (recipe below)
4 tablespoons grated low-fat Monterey Jack cheese
  (1/3 less fat)

1. Fold over each flour tortilla and paint the top half with 2 tablespoons of Smoked Fire each. Sprinkle 2 tablespoons cheese over each folded half.

2. Toast in toaster oven or under broiler for about 1 and 1/2 minutes or until cheese is bubbly and tortilla is crisp around the edges.
Makes 2 servings.

Calories	159	Protein	7 gm
Fat	3 gm	Carbohydrate	25 gm
Sodium	355 mg	Cholesterol	10 mg

SMOKED FIRE

This salsa is wonderfully complex and is likely to cause an addiction in anyone who loves extra hot food.

1 can plum tomatoes (28 ounces), drained
4 chipotle chiles en vinagre from can
4 cloves garlic

1. Place everything in a food processor and puree. This salsa will keep for a couple of weeks in the refrigerator. 14 servings

Calories	14	Protein	.6 gm
Fat	.1 gm	Carbohydrate	3 gm
Sodium	155 mg	Cholesterol	0

GRANDMA'S RICE WITH EMBELLISHMENT

When you are serving spicy main dishes Grandma's rice is a perfect accompaniment. Grandma fried her rice in a lot more olive oil to give it the toasted flavor typical of Spanish rice.

1 tablespoon olive oil
1 cup long-grain rice
1/2 cup chopped onion
1 teaspoon minced garlic
1/2 cup skinned, chopped tomato

2 and 1/2 cups water
1/2 teaspoon salt
2 teaspoons ground chile
1/2 cup chopped carrots (about 2)
1/2 cup petite frozen peas

1. Heat the olive oil in a deep 2-quart pot with a lid. Saute the rice until it gives off a whiff of a popcorn smell and is a little golden. Add the chopped onion and saute for a couple of minutes, mixing it into the rice. Add the garlic and chopped tomato and saute.

2. Add the water, salt, and ground chile. Simmer until little holes start to appear in the surface of the rice, about 10 minutes. Sprinkle the chopped carrots on top along with the peas. Put on the lid.

3. Cook the rice on low heat for 10 more minutes. Then turn off the heat and leave undisturbed for 10 more minutes.

6 servings.

Calories	157	Protein	3 gm
Fat	3 gm	Carbohydrate	30 gm
Sodium	218 mg	Cholesterol	0

LICUADOS

CHAPTER V

LICUADOS AND AQUAS FRESAS OF MEXICO

exicans, except for their consumption of lard and their national sweet tooth (even Coca Cola has to be made sweeter for them) have a diet high in carbohydrates, fruits, and vegetables. Especially healthy is their love of the fruit drinks called licuados made either with strained fruit juice and sugar or pureed whole fruits. At the very heart of the old San Miguel market, raised up on a platform, was the licuado lady with her array of various tropical fruits and several blenders. After telling her the blend of fruits you wanted, she would puree them straight up or add some milk. After a late night of sipping vino tinto in one of the cafes, my roommate and I would drag our parched mouths down to visit the licuado lady.

SAN MIGUEL MARKET LICUADO

This licuado is particularly good with a Mexican or New Mexican breakfast focused on chiles. It is loaded with beta carotene and a beautiful sunny orange color which looks best in clear glasses. The recipe doubles easily.

1/2 cup diced fresh mango
1/2 cup diced fresh pineapple
1/2 cup sliced banana
1 cup fresh orange juice
1/2 papaya nectar blend (papaya puree,
   white grape juice, and pineapple juice)

Puree everything in a blender.
2 servings.

Calories	166	Protein	2 gm
Fat	.7 gm	Carbohydrate	40 gm
Sodium	6 mg	Cholesterol	0

FRUIT RAINBOW LICUADO

In East Los Angeles licuados are a staple in many of the small family restaurants owned by Mexicans, Cubans, and Salvadorans. This is one of the most popular in the Los Burritos licuado bar. Drink this in a beautiful glass and pretend you're at a health spa.

8 ounces fresh orange juice
1/2 cup papaya nectar delight (blend of white grape juice, pineapple juice and papaya puree)
1/2 cup boysenberries or marion boysenberries, frozen
1/2 cup fresh strawberries
1/2 cup diced watermelon

1. Puree everything in a blender.
2 servings (approximately 3 cups of licuado)

Calories	126	Protein	2 gm
Fat	.6 gm	Carbohydrate	29 gm
Sodium	6 mg	Cholesterol	0

NUTTY PINEAPPLE SHAKE

This is my own idea of what a healthy licuado should be when you want it to take the place of breakfast. One of the great flavor combinations of all time is peanut butter and banana sandwiches so barring those right now, the next best thing is to do what a health spa in Napa Valley does —blend a tiny bit of nut butter into a fruit drink.

1 cup diced fresh pineapple
1/2 cup sliced banana
2 cups nonfat milk
1/2 cup nonfat yogurt
1 tablespoon almond butter (or peanut butter)
1 teaspoon vanilla
2 teaspoons honey
4 ice cubes

1. Place all of the ingredients into a blender jar and blend into a frothy shake. If you place the fruit (pineapple and banana slices) into a zip-loc bag the night before and freeze, the shake will be even frothier. This is a creamy, wonderful shake that is so good you will think it is loaded with calories.

Makes 32 ounces or 4 servings, 8 ounces each.

Calories	134	Protein	7 gm
Fat	3 gm	Carbohydrate	21 gm
Sodium	103 mg	Cholesterol	3 mg

STRAWBERRIES AND CREAM LICUADO

This licuado is not really strawberries and cream but just tastes like it. Kids love this one.

1 cup fresh strawberries, sliced
1 cup low-fat milk (2%)
1/4 cup nonfat yogurt
1/2 teaspoon pure vanilla extract
3 teaspoons sugar (or honey)
4 ice cubes

1. Place everything in a blender jar and puree until frothy. You can substitute the strawberries with fresh peaches, blueberries, or any particularly sweet fruit in season. You may also use frozen fruit which will make the drink even frothier.

2 servings. Makes 16 ounces.

Calories	127	Protein	6 gm
Fat	3 gm	Carbohydrate	20 gm
Sodium	83 mg	Cholesterol	10 mg

STRAWBERRY ORANGE LICUADO

When I lived in San Miguel de Allende spring always meant the coming of the small strawberries and the sweet, spindly asparagus. The vendor walked down the narrow, cobbled streets in the morning, yelling, "Fresas, Asparaaaaaagus!" I could never resist his cry. From the wooden tray hanging around his neck he would let me have my pick.

1 cup sliced strawberries
1 cup fresh orange juice
4 ice cubes

1. Place all of the ingredients in a blender jar and puree until frothy.

2 servings or about 3 cups.

Calories	100	Protein	1 gm
Fat	.5 gm	Carbohydrate	24 gm
Sodium	2 mg	Cholesterol	0

AGUA FRESA DE SANDIA

WATERMELON JUICE

A great deal is lost in the translation of agua fresca de sandia into watermelon juice. It is not simply juice. In Mexico, whether you are passing a Sunday in Chapultepec Park or on a street corner in a small village, you are often confronted with the huge glass barrels sparkling

163

with all colors of various fruits—the aguas frescas of which my favorite is watermelon, a Mexican hot pink juice that when served over shaved ice and eaten with a taco is a small piece of heaven. Frequently, when I have had a summer barbecue, the agua fresca of watermelon is gone before the beer. Many traditional methods of preparing aguas fresas load up with sugar. The recipe below, if prepared with sweet watermelon, does not require too much sugar.

6 cups diced watermelon
1 tablespoon reserved seeds
2 cups water
1 tablespoon sugar
Juice from 1 lime, about 1 and 1/2 tablespoons juice
Lime wedges cut from 2 limes for garnish
Chopped or shaved ice

1. Puree half the amount of watermelon with 1 cup of water. Pour into a pretty glass pitcher and then add the rest of the fruit, water, lime juice, and sugar to the blender and puree. Add this to the juice in the pitcher and then stir in the reserved seeds to make an aguas fresas properly Mexican.

2. Pour over shaved ice in clear glasses and garnish with a wedge of lime.

8 servings although 4 people usually drink it all!

Calories	45	Protein	.7 gm
Fat	.5 gm	Carbohydrate	10 gm
Sodium	2 mg	Cholesterol	0

JAMAICA

One of the most traditional, old-fashioned drinks served by Mexicans, jamaica is an infusion or tea made of steeped dried hibiscus flowers but usually served cold or over ice. It is tart like cranberry juice so it is always sweetened heavily with sugar. If it is made less strong, it does not require all the sweetening and it is still a pretty raspberry red. A very refreshing drink over ice.

4 ounces dried hibiscus flowers
1 quart hot water
1/4 cup sugar
1 quart cold water
12 ounces frozen apple juice concentrate (1 large can)

1. Using a heat-proof pitcher (not plastic) or a tea pot, pour the quart of boiling water over the flowers and steep for 10 to 15 minutes.

2. Pour through a strainer to remove flowers. Be cautious about spilling for the liquid is a staining bright red. It is best to use 2 2-quart pitchers for the mixing, dividing the liquid in half. Add sugar to the warm liquid and stir until dissolved. Then add the cold water. Blend in the frozen apple juice concentrate. This amount is just enough to sweeten the jamaica (without so much sugar) and yet not dominate the drink.

Makes 3 quarts or about 12 servings

Calories	75	Protein	.2 mg	
Fat	.1 gm	Carbohydrate	19 gm	
Sodium	11 mg	Cholesterol	0	

INDULGENCES

CHAPTER VI

INDULGENCES

E ven though many of us can speak in a very intelligent, even learned fashion about nutrition and proper diets, when given the chance we are as eager as children for a treat or an indulgence. Within this chapter I have included light and medium-weight indulgences and end with a wicked chocolate cake learned from one of the most memorable French cooks in the world. But our dessert mainstay should be fruit or a cup of French roast coffee served in a beautiful cup. If you save up for desserts, they will taste even better.

Except for holidays or birthdays, my California rancho family, with its strong Spanish traditions, never served any dessert but some form of fruit usually picked off a nearby tree. A gigantic bowl of apples, peaches, figs, apricots, or grapes was placed on the table. You were given a small plate and a knife to peel and cut your fruit. Make the eating of fruit more ceremonious.

If I spot a basket of fresh raspberries in the market, I will often splurge on them. Inevitably while waiting in line, someone will ask how I can spend so much on a little basket of berries and yet they would think nothing of spending that on a bag of store cookies. Treat yourself to things that are good for you whether it be fresh raspberries, or figs, or the summer's first white peaches. When we speak of fruit for a treat, make it very special and exotic on occasion. Serve fruit in a fanciful way for guests. I do not have the patience for tempering chocolate so I just melt a good brand of semi-sweet chocolate. Dip whole strawberries into the warm chocolate and lay on a bed of crushed ice. Turn over once. Do this no more than 30 minutes before serving but hide them!

Of course, when you do splurge on dessert, eat something wonderful rather than ordinary. Left from childhood, I have a penchant for graham crackers and I adore anything chocolate. Every six months I allow myself to send for a box of Cafe Beaujolais' (see Note) graham crackers dipped in Belgian bittersweet chocolate. The ritual for my indulgence never varies. Unless I cheat and eat two crackers. I rinse off a French crystal goblet in cold water and place it in the freezer to chill for at least an hour. One chocolate cracker sits waiting on a little plate. I remove the frosty goblet and fill it with nonfat milk (don't laugh!) and quicky rush it to the table where the cracker awaits. One bite of chocolate. One deep swallow of incredibly cold milk and so on. This splurge counts.

Note: Cafe Beaujolais is in Mendocino, California 95460

POACHED PEARS WITH AMARETTI FILLING

Poaching, when done gently and quickly, is a particularly fine way to treat pears. They remain crisp and by reducing some of the poaching liquid, you have a ready-made sauce. The filling is light and slim and tastes as though you labored for hours. The trick is to use the Dicamillo amaretti cookies (see Resources), which are some of the best.

6 Bartlett pears (do not remove skins)
3 cups of red wine like Burgundy
2 cups water
1/2 cup frozen apple juice concentrate
3/4 cup sugar
2 teaspoons cinnamon
4 cloves
1 cinnamon stick

For filling:
3/4 cup part-skim milk ricotta
2 tablespoons light cream cheese
2 tablespoons powdered sugar
1 teaspoon vanilla
4 amaretti cookies, crushed to a powder
Cinnamon powder for sprinkling
Mint leaves for garnish

1. Wash the pears well. From the bottom of each pear, use a paring knife to cut out a small cavity, including most of core. You only need to remove about 1 tablespoon of pear meat.

2. In a 3-quart pot, place the wine, water, apple juice concentrate, sugar, cinnamon, cloves, and cinnamon stick. Bring to a simmer and add the pears. Simmer for 12 minutes with lid partially on. Turn the pears every couple of minutes.

3. Remove the pears to a deep dish. Pour out half of the liquid and discard. Reduce the remaining liquid on medium heat for 15 minutes to concentrate to 1 and 1/2 cups wine syrup. Pour over pears.

4. For filling, place ricotta, cream cheese, powdered sugar, and vanilla in bowl of food processor and process until smooth and creamy. Place cookies between folded sheet of wax paper. Crush by moving a rolling pin back

and forth. This works better than spinning in the food processor. Add the cookie crumbs to the rest of the filling and blend.

5. Spoon about a tablespoon of filling into the cavity of each pear. Place standing up on dessert plates and spoon about 3 tablespoons of wine syrup over each pear, sprinkle with cinnamon, and add a mint leaf to each stem. 6 servings

Calories	327	Protein	5 gm
Fat	5 gm	Carbohydrate	70 gm
Sodium	87 mg	Cholesterol	13 mg

APPLE BLUEBERRY CRISP

Cobblers and crisps usually have a great deal of butter but this one is quite delicious with an absolute mini-umum of fat. It was inspired by a crisp made by Chef David del Nagro at the Oaks Spa in Ojai, California.

1 package frozen blueberries, 16 ounces
1 quart cored, chopped apples (about 3 large)
2 teaspoons cinnamon
2 tablespoon brown sugar
1/2 cup frozen apple juice concentrate
2 teaspoons arrowroot for thickener
1 cup rolled oats
1/2 cup finely ground graham crackers
2 tablespoons brown sugar
2 tablespoons melted corn oil margarine
1 tablespoon frozen apple juice concentrate, thawed

1. Combine the blueberries, chopped apples, cinnamon, and brown sugar. In a microwave on high power, heat the apple juice concentrate and the arrowroot for 70 seconds until thickened. Stir with a fork about halfway through the cooking. Add the thickened juice to the mixed fruit.

2. For the topping, combine the oats, graham crackers, brown sugar, melted margarine, and thawed apple juice concentrate. Stir together until well-blended.

3. Pour fruit into a 13" x 7 and 1/2" baking dish. Sprinkle crumbs over the top. Bake in a preheated 350 degree oven for 40 minutes.

8 servings

Calories	218	Protein	26 gm
Fat	5 gm	Carbohydrate	43 gm
Sodium	86 mg	Cholesterol	0

STRAWBERRY MERINGUE SHORTCAKES

These cakes are not the regular dry, crisp meringues but bear a resemblance to the Pavlova, the national dessert of Australia. The centers are soft and creamy, a perfect foil for unsweetened strawberries.

6 egg whites, room temperature
1/8 teaspoon salt
1 and 1/2 cups sugar (superfine is best)
1 tablespoon cider vinegar

2 teaspoons vanilla extract
1 quart of sliced strawberries
1/2 cup whipping cream
1 tablespoon powdered sugar
1 teaspoon vanilla extract

1. Using the whisk attachment of an electric mixer, beat the egg whites and salt until soft peaks form. Begin adding the sugar by the tablespoon. Add about 1 tablespoon every 30 seconds. After half of the sugar has been added, add the vanilla. Continue with the sugar additions and then whip in the vinegar. The mixture will be very stiff.

2. On 2 baking sheets lined with baking parchment, place 10 dollops of meringue. Smooth them out into 4 and 1/2 inch circles.

3. Bake in a preheated 250 degree oven for only 40 minutes. The meringue shortcakes should remain pale white and soft in the center with a thin crisp shell on the outside. Make sure that your oven is not hotter than 250 degrees. Removed the meringues from the oven and leave them on the baking sheets to cool.

4. Just before serving time, whip the cream with the powdered sugar and vanilla just until soft peaks form. Spoon 1/2 cup of strawberries over each meringue shortcake, spooning on a tablespoon of whipped cream. If you think you would like to be more generous with the

cream, you'll have to double the amount given above but this amount will not be included in the nutritional ana lysis.

10 servings

Calories	186	Protein	3 gm
Fat	4 gm	Carbohydrate	36 gm
Sodium	65 mg	Cholesterol	13 mg

STRAWBERRY BROWNIE PIZZA

Three of these brownie pizzas at the opening of an art exhibit were swamped immediately and gone within minutes.

1/2 cup melted butter
2 eggs
1/2 cup brown sugar
1/4 cup sugar
2 teaspoons vanilla
3/4 cup sweet ground chocolate (Ghiradelli)
1/4 teaspoon salt
2/3 cup unsifted flour
8 ounces light cream cheese, softened
1/4 cup powdered sugar
1 teaspoon vanilla extract
10 strawberries
1/4 cup semi-sweet chocolate chips, melted

1. Cut a piece of parchment to fit a 12-inch pizza pan and preheat oven to 350 degrees.

2. Beat the eggs one at a time into the melted butter (or use margarine if you like), next add the brown sugar and regular sugar. Beat well to blend. Then add the vanilla, the ground chocolate, salt, and flour. If you do not have Ghiradelli chocolate, substitute 1/2 cup ground bitter cocoa and 1/4 cup powdered sugar. Mix everything together but do not overblend.

3. Pour brownie batter out onto the pizza pan and spread to the edges. Bake for approximately 14 minutes. Remove and allow the brownie to cool on the pan.

4. Beat the cream cheese, powdered sugar, and vanilla together. Spread over the brownie pizza. Slice the strawberries from top to bottom. Arrange in pinwheel fashion around the brownie, starting with the pointed ends of the strawberries facing outward. When the brownie pizza is covered with strawberries, drizzle the melted chocolate artistically over the surface. By grabbing the edge of the parchment paper, slide the brownie pizze onto a flat serving platter. Cut into wedges to serve.

12 servings

Calories	247	Protein	5 gm
Fat	14 gm	Carbohydrate	29 gm
Sodium	244 mg	Cholesterol	66 mg

NORMA'S ELEGANT PERSIMMON

In every book I have done, my dear friend Norma has one of her best recipes, kind of like breaking a bottle of champagne over the ship's prow before the maiden voyage. She only eats dessert if it is fruit or if it is uncommonly good so I trust her greatly.

1 perfectly ripe persimmon
2 tablespoons good brandy or Grand Marnier

1. Freeze persimmon for several hours.

2. Just 20 minutes before serving, slice persimmon in paper thin pieces using a serrated knife. Hopefully, the fruit should still be crystalline. Place on a dessert plate and drizzle with the Grand Marnier. Serve immediately because you want it to taste like persimmon sorbet. Serves 1. If you need more, freeze 1 persimmon per person.

Calories	114	Protein	.20 gm
Fat	.10 gm	Carbohydrate	17 gm
Sodium	.25 mg	Cholesterol	0

SIMCA'S CHOCOLATE ALMOND CAKE

It never fails. Everytime I serve this cake, I'm told that I could open a restaurant and serve only this cake. Many years ago, at the High Tree Farm in Napa Valley, Simone Beck taught 8 rapt students, including myself, how to make this special dessert. The cake is barely held together with ground almonds and so upon cooking, it falls and cracks. Simca covered these cracks with a divine icing. A few months ago, when I had frozen an extra cake without icing, I made one of those earth-shattering discoveries. My husband and I were dying for a piece of cake. We removed the frozen cake from the freezer and cut out 2 wedges with a sharp knife, placing them each on a plate. Intending to thaw the cake enough to sink our teeth into, I zapped each wedge in a micro-wave oven for only 20 seconds. The cake became soft and oozy on the inside and remained crisp on the outside. Heavenly. Sprinkled with powdered sugar to make it look pretty, the warm cake doesn't even miss the icing. The nutritional analysis below includes the icing.

1/4 cup brandy
1/4 cup raisins
7 ounces semi-sweet chocolate
3 tablespoons water
1/2 cup sweet butter, softened
3 eggs, separated
1/2 cup sugar
1/3 cup sugar to be added to egg whites at soft peaks
4 and 1/2 tablespoons cake flour
2/3 cup finely ground almonds
1/8 teaspoon salt
Chocolate Icing:
4 ounces semi-sweet chocolate
1/4 cup expresso coffee or strong coffee
4 tablespoons softened sweet butter

1. Soak the brandy and raisins together, preferably at least a hour before starting cake. Grease a 9-inch cake pan and line with parchment. Grease the parchment.

2. Melt chocolate with water over low heat or in microwave. Watch and stir. Now place in a mixer bowl. With the beater attachment running slowly, add pieces of the soft butter. Mix until pieces of chocolate and butter are blended. Now add egg yolks, one at a time. Next add the 1/2 cup of sugar.

2. Blend the flour and ground almonds together. (Note: if you do not have a processor to grind the almonds, often you can find an excellent almond powder in health food stores) Alternately add the brandy and raisins and the flour-almond combination to the cake batter.

3. Beat the egg whites with the pinch of salt until soft peaks form and then slowly add the 1/3 cup of sugar. Beat until stiff. Add some of the whites to the cake batter to lighten and then add the rest of the whites by gently folding.

4. Pour the batter into the cake pan. Bake for about 27 minutes. You want the center of the cake to remain very moist but crisp on the outside. The top will crack as the cake cools down. Don't worry. This is the way it is supposed to be. If the cake is unevenly cracked just push down the cracks as if you were patting it smooth.

5. If you want to serve the cake as suggested above, just wrap well in plastic wrap and freeze for several hours or overnight (or for a month). Cut into wedges with a serrated knife. Place each piece on a heat-proof dessert plate. Using high power, zap in the microwave for 20 seconds each. Do not try to heat the cake in a regular oven which will only heat from the exterior.

6. Or frost the cake with the Chocolate Icing. Melt the chocolate with the coffee. Blend in the sweet butter. Spread icing over sides and then top of cake.
Serves 8

Calories	532	Protein	6 gm
Fat	37 gm	Carbohydrate	51 gm
Sodium	63mg	Cholesterol	126 mg

INDEX

Spicy Split Pea Soup, 60
Cheese
Black Bean Soup, 97
Corn Enchiladas, 117
Eggplant Enchiladas, 144
Elegant Taco Salad, 17
Green Chicken Enchiladas, 119
Layered Pesto Cheese, 35
Low-Class Taco Salad, 20
Quesadilla, 155
Vegetable Burrito, 137
Chicken
Caldo de Tlalpeño, 54
Chicken Chile, 123
Chicken Rapido, 151
Chicken Tostada, 11
Chicken Colorado, 140
Green Chicken Enchiladas, 119
Janet's Chicken Soup, 45
Pan de Maiz, 122
Pasadena Chicken Tostada, 13
Posole, 108
Soft Tacos, 152
Sopa de Lima, 47
Toasted Sopa de Tortilla, 63
Chicken Breast
Perfect Poached, 12
Chicken Broth
Easy Friendly, 42
Really Easy, 44
Chile Sauce
For Corn Enchiladas, 117
Killer Red Sauce, 139
Chili
Black Bean Chili, 95
Bouillabaise Chili, 86
Chicken Chili, 123
Dynamite Vegetarian Chili, 95

Lentil Chili, 104
Chipotle
Baja California Tacos, 80
Black Bean Chili, 70
Grilled Yucatan Fish, 79
Smoked Fire 156
Turkey Chipotle Tostada, 8
Chocolate
Simca's Chocolate Almond
  Cake, 179
Strawberry Brownie Pizza, 176
Corn
Brown Rice Lentil Salad, 115
Corn Enchiladas, 117
Chicken Chili, 123
Dynamite Vegetarian Chili, 95
Green Corn Tamales, 119
Mexican Vegetable Soup, 65
New Mexican Potato Salad, 34
Pan de Maiz, 122
Pasadena Chicken Tostada, 13
Rancho Colache, 113
Sopa de Maiz, 73
Tamale Pie, 111
Cornmeal
Black Bean Pancakes, 100
Green Corn Tamales, 119
Pan de Maiz, 122
Tamale Pie, 111
Cucumbers
Basque Salad, 28
Mexican Gazpacho, 72
Eggplant
Enchiladas, 144
Enchiladas
Corn, 117
Eggplant, 144
Green Chicken, 145

183

RESOURCES

THE CHILE SHOP
109 E. Water St., Santa Fe, New
Mexico 87501 505-983-6080
One of best sources for dried chiles,
Dixon and Chimayo, dried posole, and
blue corn.

CHILE PEPPER EMPORIUM
328 San Felipe Rd. N.W.
Albuquerque (Old Town)
New Mexico 87104
505-242-7538
Dried chiles, dried posole, beans, and
Care packages from Southwest.

THE GREEN CHILE FIX CO.
P.O. Box 5463
Santa Fe, New Mexico 87502
Wonderful dried green chile great to use
as a spice. Dried Chipotles.

NATIVE SEEDS/SEARCH
2509 N. Campbell Ave. #325
Tucson, Arizona 85719
Dried beans of all kinds.

PEPPERS
4009 N. Brown Ave.
Scottsdale, Arizona85251
602-990-8347
Sandia chile, anchos, dried posole.

COBBLE AND MICKLE
2228 S.W. 21st Ave.
Portland, Oregon 97201
Cookbooks

SANTA FE SCHOOL OF COOKING
116 W. San Francisco St.
Santa Fe, New Mexico 87501
505-983-4511
Southwestern cooking classes. Ship
green chiles in season.

PENDERY'S OF TEXAS
1-800-533-1870
The most expansive selection of dried
herbs, spices, and Mexican ingredients.

BARGETTO SOQUEL WINERY
Soquel, Ca. 95073
Produce fine red and white wine
vinegars (90 grain).

AIDELL SAUSAGE COMPANY
1575 Minnosota St.
San Francisco, Ca.
415-285-6660
Homemade-style chorizo, Cajun tasso
ham, and other wonderful sausage.

DICAMILLO BAKERY
811 Linwood Ave.
Niagara Falls, N.Y. 14305
Produce my favorite amaretti cookie
and biscotti di vino. Sold in fine
grocery stores.